The Forgotten Rivals
The History of Bootle Football Club
1880 - 93

Tony Onslow

First Published 2005 by Countyvise Limited,
14 Appin Road, Birkenhead, Wirral CH41 9HH

Copyright © 2005 Tony Onslow

The right of Tony Onslow to be identified as the author of this work has been asserted by his in accordance with the Copyright, Design and Patents Act 1988.

British Library Cataloguing in Publication Data.
A catalogue record for this book is available from the British Library.

ISBN 1 901231 54 2

All rights reserved. No part of this publication may be reproduced, stored in a retrieval system, or transmitted, in any other form, or by any other means, electronic, chemical, mechanic, photocopying, recording or otherwise, without the prior permission of the publisher.

The Bootle Introduction

Tucked away amid the noise of traffic and urban development Bootle cricket ground continues to move along with the times. A new glass fronted pavilion looks proudly out over the square playing field and on to the houses beyond. On a hot summer's day the Hawthorne Road ground offers the local cricket fans a peaceful haven in which to watch the game. This ground however once echoed the roars of thousands of people who watched a completely different sport.

Bootle Association Football Club once used the ground to stage their home matches and challenge neighbours Everton to be the top team on Merseyside. Beginning life as Bootle St Johns in 1880 the club played on various locations before eventually, along with the local cricket club, they settled at the present day location. By importing players from Wales and Scotland the club soon became capable of matching the finest teams in the kingdom. In 1888 neighbours, and rivals Everton, were elected to the football league thus guaranteeing them a regular source of revenue from matches against the top clubs of the day. Left out in the cold, Bootle began a period of gradual decline as the quality fixtures offered by Everton drew away the local football fans from their ground. The club however struggled on gallantly and in 1892 were elected as founder members of the football league division two.

Despite this new venture Bootle, laying in the close proximity of the best supported team in the land, could not compete. Faced with dwindling crowds they folded after just one year in the football league. This book chronicles their formative years, subsequent development, and their desperate battle to survive.

Acknowledgements

I would like to thank my wife Joan and my son Alex for all the support they have given to me in completing this book. I would also like to thank the library staff at Liverpool and Crosby local history departments for all their help and kind consideration. Finally, Margaret May at the Mitchall Library, Glasgow who helped me find Andrew Watson.

Dedication

This book is dedicated to the memory of my late friend, Eric Palmer

The Early Years

When the congregation of St Johns Church, Bootle welcomed a new Deacon into their parish they had no indication of the impact that this young man was about to make on the development of their community. The newcomer, Alfred Keely, was about to introduce the local population to the pleasures that were derived from the game of association football.

The son of a successful Merchant, Alfred William Johnson Keely, had been born in Nottinghamshire in the year 1854. Along with his younger brother Edwin, he had attended Shrewsbury school before entering St Johns College, Cambridge. Here he was awarded a B.A in 1874. Deciding on a career in the church he studied for a further three years before being ordained at Chester in 1877. Alfred was then placed under the guidance of the Reverend R W Beardsley at St Johns, Bootle where he was ordained in 1879.

Alfred, during his days at Cambridge, took part in the many sporting activities that were available. One of the games, association football, had been slowly developing at the university since 1863 and now processed a printed code of rules; Alfred Keely brought his love of the association game with him to St Johns, Bootle.

It was a time of "Muscular Christian" when Reverend Keely, aged 23, arrived on Merseyside where he quickly introduced this method of theology to the young men within the parish. He found however that the Bootle area was given over to the code of rugby football and no association clubs were in existence.

Reverend Keely was informed that disciples of the round ball game could be seen playing each Saturday at the nearby Stanley Park. Travelling in that direction he found, to his delight, that association football was indeed to be found in the north end of Liverpool and that several teams were already in existence. He returned to Bootle and, with the help of certain friends, founded Bootle St Johns AFC.

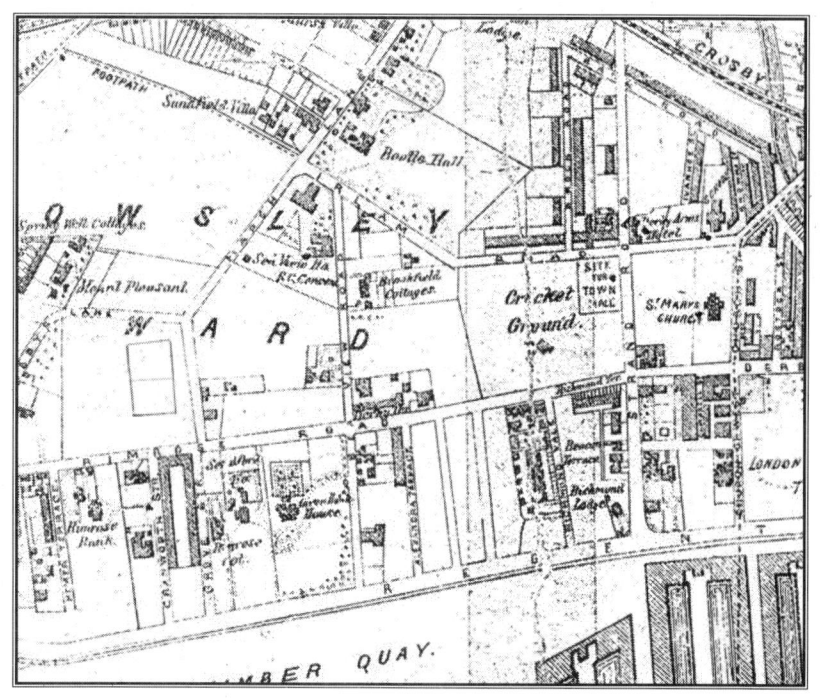

Map of Bootle 1880. Left Location of Bootle's first ground at Bibbys Lane

The new club used the remaining winter months to collect enough players to place two teams in the field. With the new season approaching they managed to secure a playing pitch on Bibbys Lane. The area, formerly known as Bootle Marsh, had slowly been irrigated and was now ideally suited as a level playing field. The huge Gladstone Dock complex had yet to be constructed and on a bleak winter's afternoon the area could be anything but inviting. After a couple of warm up matches amongst the club members, Bootle St Johns football club was ready for action.

On 20th October 1880 Bootle St Johns arrived at Stanley Park to play their first ever association football match against Everton. The team line-up was Rev A W Keely, goal, J Masheder, back, J Betts and C Allsopp, half backs, E R Keely, S Keely, Gosson, A Allsop, Skillicorn, Woods and Reverend Chapman, forwards. Bootle won the toss and elected to play with the wind in their favour.

The first half was a dull affair and at half time neither side had scored. During the second half the superior play of the visitors began to show. The home side, made up of local players, began to struggle against the style of play demonstrated by the public school players in the Bootle team. Edwin and Sam Keely, both of them brothers of Alfred, each scored two goals as Bootle St John's triumphed 4-0.

The next team to visit Bibbys Lane was Birkenhead FC. Amongst their ranks was a certain Welshman named Robert E Lythgoe who had recently been transferred to the Merseyside area with his job. Bob Lythgoe, who had formerly played association football in the Wrexham area, had taken up residence in Kirkdale. He was later to play for Bootle.

The game against Birkenhead was very much in the favour of Bootle. The home side, with their public school players, proved too much for the visitors to handle. Two goals by Reverend Keely and one by his brother Edwin gave Bootle a 3-0 victory.

Bootle now became the first side from the Merseyside area to enter the Lancashire County Cup. After obtaining a home tie with Num Nook (Accrington) the club was granted permission to play the tie on the ground of the Bootle cricket club at Irlam Road. The new venture ended in failure as Bootle lost 3-1.

Bootle next faced a side called "The Liverpool Association". Formed by local solicitor Edwin Berry, the team was, in all probability, the first in Liverpool to play football under the association rules. The game, which took place at Newsham Park, saw the Reverend Keely score all the goals in a 3-0 win for Bootle.

The well-appointed members of the ·Bootle team then paid a visit to the accident border town of Shrewsbury. Here they played a game against the pupils of the local Public School The Twist Brothers, former players with Oxford University, were in the Bootle ranks as the teams lined up on the picturesque school playing field. The visitors had arrived with only nine men and had to borrow two players from the school. The game, which was evenly contested, ended in a goal-less draw.

Somewhere around the Christmas period the suffix of St Johns was dropped and the name became simply Bootle. The first team encountered under this new name was Newton Heath. The Manchester club, making their first trip to Merseyside, lost to Bootle 3-0. Next weekend Bootle, with goals from Rev Keely,

Hill and Henstock, registered a 3-0 away victory over Manchester Wanderers at Brooks Bar.

On 5th March 1881 Bootle, struggling to field a side, arrived at Stanley Park to face Everton with only eight men. Three of the spectators, conversant with the rules of association football, kindly consented to place their services at the disposal of the visitors. All parties concerned agreed to the arrangement and the Reverend Keely kicked off for Bootle. The visitors, facing a full strength Everton side, contributed to a spirited and well-contested game. The outcome of the game was decided by a single goal that was scored in favour of Everton by Knightly.

Further games against St Peters (Kirkdale) and Bolton Wanderers "A" led on to the last game of the season against Blackburn Olympic. The game, played during the Easter Holiday, saw Bootle take the field at Bibbys Lane with a weak side. They were well beaten by 7-0.

Season 1881-82

Bootle football club was now beginning to find favour with the local dignitaries of the area and began the season with a full list of officers. The honourable president was Mr. W Poulson JP, the Mayor of Bootle; Mr. W Gibson JP was president. The vice-presidents were, Mr.Chas Taylor JP, Mr. JP McArthur JP, Mr. G Barnes JP, and Mr. TP Danson JP. Dr Herbert Taylor was the Captain. Mr. R M Sloan was Hon. Secretary and Mr. F G Heaton filled the roll of Hon. Treasurer. The committee was made up of Rev A W Keely, F Henstock, E. V. Rayner, E. Bell, A.A. Allsop, R E Lythgoe, and J Rodgers.

The season began with three home fixtures against Manchester Wanderers, Bolton Wanderers and Blackpool before playing an away match against Stoke at the Victoria Ground. Bootle then became the first club from the Merseyside area to enter the national FA Cup contest.

Their opponents were a team of former students called Blackburn Law Society and Bootle experienced some difficulty when trying to arrange the fixture. In order to place their strongest team in the field, the club was forced to encounter two matches on the same day The FA Cup-tie, which took seniority, was played on the cricket ground at Irlam Road. First half goals from Smith and G W Turner gave the home side the lead but a late goal from the visitors made for an anxious finish. Bootle held on to win the tie 2-1.

The Bootle players, after taking a brief recess then lined up to face Preston North End in a Lancashire cup-tie. Bootle took the lead before the endeavours of the day began to show in their play. Preston slowly got on top and soon secured an equalizing goal. However the dark November skies began to close in and very soon it was dark The teams, having played for one hour, decided to leave the field and declare the game a draw. Bootle lost the re-play at Deepdale 2-1.

The second round of the FA cup gave Bootle an away tie at Turton. The day began badly when three members of the team failed to catch the appropriate train from Kirkdale railway station. The rest of the team, changing trains at Bolton, soon arrived at their intended destination.

(Turton, the oldest football club in Lancashire, had been formed under the guidance of the local Kaye family. After acquiring great wealth from the cotton trade the family had sent their three sons to be educated at Harrow school. On returning home the eldest boy John, helped by local schoolmaster, W T Dixon, formed an association football team. The club were later acknowledged as the original custodians of the association rules in Lancashire. From this industrial hamlet, set in a deep cleft on the Lancashire moors, the game of association football spread like wild fire through the larger towns of the county.)

The Bootle team arrived to be greeted by the Turton club officials before being escorted to their headquarters at the

Cheetham Arms. The eight Bootle players, led by Bob Lythgoe, took the field before a fair crowd who were assembled on the home ground at Tower Street. The visitors, hopelessly outnumbered, were forced on to the defensive and conceded three goals in the first half. During the interval two of the lost Bootle players arrived and quickly took their place in the team. The game however was now beyond the visitors who lost 4-0.

On the 14th of January Bootle met Everton at Bibbys Lane. The Reverend Keely took charge in the middle as Everton, watched by five hundred people, began the game against the slight breeze. The home side made a confident start and took the lead when a stumble by G Bargary in the Everton goal allowed in J Baxter to score. The rest of the game however belonged to Jack M'Gill of Everton. The former Glasgow Rangers player scored a brace of goals each side of the interval to give the visitors a 4-1 victory. After the game the Bootle committee entertained the sides at the Derby Arms Hotel.

Queen Park Strollers, the second eleven from the famous Glasgow club, arrived to face Bootle during the Easter holiday. The fixture could be considered by some to be a little strange as earlier in the season the Queens Park first eleven had declined an invitation to travel south. The Glasgow side, when drawn against Accrington in the FA cup, had granted the Lancashire side a first round walkover.

The energetic home committee did all in their power to make the Scots welcome. The game, played at Irlam Road, was watched by the largest football crowd yet to assemble on Merseyside. Nearly all the prominent members of the local association clubs were seen to be amongst the attendance of over one thousand. A great cheer greeted the appearance on the ground of the famous black and white hooped shirts.

Those who expected a one sided affair were quickly surprised by the exceptional play of the Bootle side. For the first half-hour of the game the home defence held firm until the Scots took the lead with a goal from Harrower. Five minutes from the end the same player scored again to give the visitors a hard earned 2-0 victory.

Season 1882-83

The summer of 1882 was to prove eventful and threaten the very existence of Bootle Football Club. The guidance of Reverend Keely was lost to them when the church hierarchy transferred him to a new parish in Wimbledon.

(After leaving Bootle, Reverend Keely went on to dedicate his life to the Church of England and serve it faithfully to the close. Spending one year at Wimbledon he moved first to Surbition and then Cowes, Isle of Wight before taking over the parish of St Paul's in Huddersfield. He remained in Yorkshire until 1917 from where, along with his wife Beatrice, he moved and became Rector of Orlingbury, Northants. In 1922 he retired to the Cotswolds and took up residence in the tiny village of Minchinhampton from where, at the age of 74, he departed this world in April 1939. His funeral, attended by several local dignities, took place at Minchinhampton parish church from where he was laid to rest in the local churchyard. The time of his death spared him from the horrors of the World War two and the destruction of his beloved St Johns church. In 1941 the building was demolished during a German air raid.)

The loss suffered to Bootle by the departure of Reverend Keely was compounded by the decision of the former Eton and

Harrow players to also leave the club. Finding a base at the Aigburth Hotel and a pitch on the adjoining field the former public school men went on to form a team which they called, Liverpool Ramblers.

With the ground on Bibbys Lane now needed for development Bootle were forced to vacate the area and seek pastures new. A suitable playing field was then acquired near to the Salisbury Hotel on Marsh Lane.

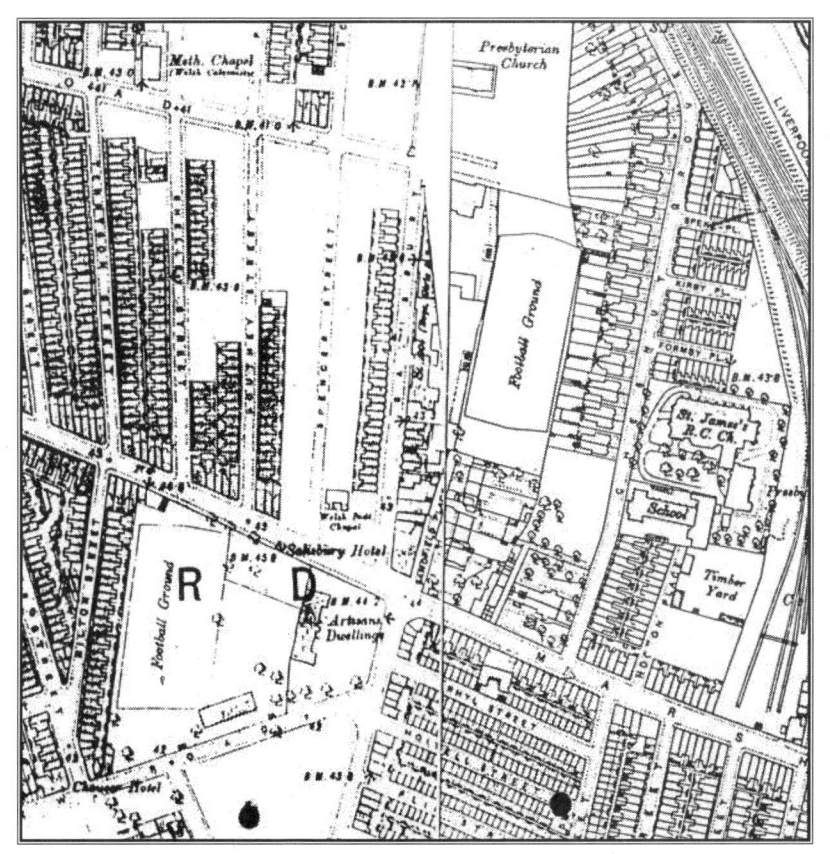

The second Bootle home ground on Marsh Lane

With help from several good quality Welsh players, introduced by Bob Lythgoe, Bootle began the season by opposing Liverpool Ramblers in their inaugural match. The crowd at Marsh Lane was small on account of events elsewhere. Blackburn Rovers, the losing FA cup finalists, were making their first visit to Liverpool in order to play the Liverpool Association at the nearby Walton Stiles. (Blackburn won the game 10-1)

Liverpool Ramblers responded to the Welsh challenge by introducing a certain Henry A Chursham into their ranks. A former pupil at Repton Public School, Chursham returned to native Nottingham, and played for both Forest and County. Finally committing himself to County he scored his first FA cup against Derbyshire FC in 1880 before going on to amass a record forty eight goals in the tournament. He also won eight international caps for England.

When the play commenced Bootle took an early lead and led for most of the game. With minutes remaining the Ramblers scored a goal which, on a plea of off side, was objected to by Bootle. There being no referee to give a decision, the final outcome of the game could not be decided.

On 23rd September Bootle struggled to raise a side to travel to meet Accrington. Their plight was eased by the kind help of Everton players Frank Brettle and Jack M'Gill who, having no game that day, kindly consented to turn out to help Bootle. The two sides proved to be worlds apart as the East Lancashire side won by 12 goals to 0 The match took place at Thornyholme Cricket ground and ended in adversity for Everton. Jack M. Gill, who had an outstanding game, was later induced to sign for Accrington.

Early in December local rivals Everton made their first visit to the new location on Marsh Lane. Bootle, who began the game with ten men, included Bob Lythgoe who was assisted up front by guest player J M'Innis. Facing a strong wind the home side took an early lead with a goal from Grayson. The missing player, Rod Ashton from Darwen, now put in an appearance and brought the home side number up to its full complement. The rest of the game was an even affair that was finally settled in favour of Bootle with a late second goal courtesy of Ashton.

The fashion of the time was to play host to one of the many Scottish clubs who toured England during their New Year holiday. On 2nd January Bootle received a visit from a team playing under the unusual name of "Luton of Glasgow". The game was played at Irlam Road and ended in a 3-3 draw

The most famous and much publisized game between Everton and Bootle took place at Stanley Park on 20th January 1883. The encounter was however, at its best exciting, and at its worst disorganized. The local newspapers reports contain no reference to anybody being subjected to physical violence.

To complement the occasion Bob Lythgoe bolstered the Bootle side with one or two class acquisitions. These were Scotsman J M'Innes and English International, J Brodie from Wolverhampton Everton played only club members.

When the game began, a crowd of around one and a half thousand surrounded the pitch. The two sides then produced an exciting first half that produced chances at both ends. Minutes before the break the first major incident occurred.

The ball was near the Bootle goal when one of the Everton men, unfortunately for his side, claimed one of the Bootle players had handled the ball. (The penalty kick was not yet in force.) Before the referee could sound his whistle, Morris scored for Everton. The Bootle players, having stopped playing, appealed to the umpire, who informed the referee of the infringement. The goal was then disallowed. The Bootle defence then repelled the free kick and at half time the score was 0-0.

Everton, disappointed by the decision, went behind on the hour to a goal from Alfred Allsop The home side fought hard to save the game without success. With just minutes remaining, a second confrontation occurred.

A shot from Ashton grazed the Everton crossbar. (It is highly likely that the bar was in fact a piece of the tape and this could have led to the dispute). Bootle claimed a goal but the Everton players fervently objected. Mayhem then ensued.

The spectators, invading the field in their hundreds, surrounded the referee who was lost for a time in the crowd. The play however continued and Everton kicked the ball up field, Harry Williams, running on to clearance, placed the ball between the Bootle posts. The referee, who did not see what had taken place, could not make a decision and the game ended in a most unsatisfactory manner.

(This game was without a doubt a watershed in the early development of association football on Merseyside. In future all clubs would be answerable to a new governing body. The committee of "The Liverpool and District Football Association" would now settle all disputes that arose between the member clubs.)

The FA Cup draw presented Bootle with an away tie against one of the strongest teams in Lancashire, Bolton Wanderers. The visitors, arriving at Trinity Street railway station, were warmly welcomed by their hosts and conveyed to the club headquarters at the Gladstone Arms. Here they changed before making their way to Pikes Lane: (Today known as Deane Road).

The visitors found the Bolton ground to be a large square enclosure that was also used for cricket It contained a small wooden stand and a high grass bank that contained a rudiment of terracing. There was a hurricane force wind blowing as both captains met in the middle, before a crowd estimated at two thousand. The all-important flip of the coin was benevolent to Bolton who quite naturally chose to play the first half with the elements in their favour.

The Bootle defenders, up against it from the start, were soon buried under a first half avalanche of Bolton pressure. Struthers, a recent acquisition from Glasgow Rangers, was the main protagonist who helped himself to three of the four goals that were scored by the home side during the first half. So consistent was the Bolton pressure that Wilson, the home goalkeeper, felt confident enough to leave the home timbers under the protection of the strong wind and join in the out field play.

With the game now beyond them, Bootle started the second half brightly and, with a goal from Roberts, reduced the arrears. The extreme physical exertions required in completing the first half, proved too much for the visitors. Two more goals from Struthers increased the home tally as Bootle lost 6-1.

With their future hanging in the balance Bootle was now reduced to playing one or two minor local games, before a young Welsh medical student came to their aid. Dr Eyton Jones, an associate of Bob Lythgoe, had recently joined the club after taking up a position at Birkenhead Hospital. He was a leading amateur who had already played for his country and his acquisition improved the status of the club.

With St Benedict's providing the opposition, Bootle played their first tie in the new Liverpool Cup competition. The game took place at Irlam Road and was won by Bootle. The same venue was engaged one week later where a crowd of one thousand welcomed the return visit of the Queens Park Strollers. Bootle gave a good account of their playing qualities but lost to the only goal of the game that was scored by Brock.

Bootle, after next beating Earlestown, now faced Everton in the semi-final of the Liverpool Cup. The match was played on Liverpool College playing field at Fairfield. The location (today the home of Merseyside Police) was firmly enclosed by a strong brick wall and enjoyed the benefit of a fine pavilion. It was possibly the best-suited venue to stage the event as the expanding public transport system passed the ground. The location could also be reached by train when alighting at Stanley railway station.

The teams lined up on a sunny day before a disappointing crowd of around five hundred people (The Grand National was run on the same day at Aintree). The pitch, though a little narrow, was in excellent condition. Bootle won the toss and chose to defend the Prescot Road goal. The first half was very much in favour of Bootle. Attacking from the start they soon went ahead with a goal from Britten. The same player, with a fine pass, then provided a second goal that was scored by Grayson. Grayson then secured his second goal to give Bootle a 3-0 lead before the teams then changed ends.

Everton had the better of the second half but victory was now beyond them. However they did live in hope for a while when Cartwright, from a free kick, reduced the arrears. Nevertheless the day belonged to Bootle. They kept their composure to reach the final with a 3-1 victory.

Good Friday found Bootle in Llangollen to fulfil a fixture against Berwyn Rangers. Bob Lythgoe, who organized the occasion, reinforced the home side with the introduction of several local international players from the nearby Druids of Ruabon. The game was played on a hillside pitch that overlooked the river Dee. A cheerful holiday crowd watched the home side win 1-0.

Next day Bootle, placing a moderate side in the field, won an away match at Southport. On Easter Monday the newly formed Corinthians took to the field at Irlam Road.

(The London based club had been formed under the guidance of N A Jackson a leading official with the FA. The make up of the team consisted of players with proven ability that hailed from a well-appointed background. Mr Jackson hoped to develop a side to rival Queens Park, who were at the time, providing the backbone of a Scottish national team who had inflicted a series of heavy defeats on England. If England were to match the teamwork displayed by the Scots they needed to forsake their individual style of play and construct a new one based on superior teamwork. The Corinthians were formed on an arrangement similar to the present day Barbarians Rugby team and had no ground of their own.)

The morning snowfall was still in evidence as a large and inquisitive crowd lined the field to greet their distinguished visitors. Several of the leading Corinthians, (who were on an extended tour of the North) sat the game out but the visiting line-up remained impressive. First choice England goalkeeper, Harry Abermarle Swepstone (London Pilgrims) was included in the team along with Andrew Watson, the first black soccer player to be seen on Merseyside.

(Andrew Watson had been born in Guyana in 1857 and was the son of a local woman and a Scottish sugar merchant. The circumstances that brought him to Britain are as yet unclear but in 1875, he enrolled at Glasgow University to study the Arts. While playing association football in Glasgow for Parkgrove FC Andrew was asked to sign for Queen's Park and made his debut against Vale of Leven on the 24 April 1880. During his first spell at Queens Park he won three caps for Scotland. He captained his adopted country before moving South in 1882. While living in London he played for the Swifts FC from where he was invited to join the elite ranks of the Corinthians.)

The Corinthians casually took the field with their hands in their pockets. The long sleeves of their white shirts hung loose and were unbuttoned in the style of a public school football player.

The home side, refusing to be overawed by the occasion, held their ground during the early exchanges. Soon the class of the visitors began to show and Jessop gave them a first half lead.

The change of ends placed the wind and sun to the advantage of the Corinthians. Throughout the second half the Southerners continued to hold the sway and confirmed their victory with a late second goal from Morice.

The college ground at Fairfield was again the venue when Bootle met Liverpool Ramblers in the final of the Liverpool Cup. On a cold and sunny day the two sides lined up to face each other before the largest football crowd yet to assemble in Liverpool. The Ramblers, firm favourites, won the toss and chose to kick off with the oblique wind in their favour. Bootle, slightly against the early play, took the lead with a goal from Ashton. The Ramblers then sprung into life and Metcalfe turned in a long two-handed throw (now obligatory) from Stewart-Brown to put his side level. Ramblers then applied more pressure on the Bootle goal but, at half-time the score remained at 1-1.

When ends were changed Bootle had the elements in their favour and soon made their advantage tell. Ashton, having a fine game up front, went on to score a hat trick as Bootle took the trophy with a 3-1 victory.

Season 1883-84

The season was to prove a transition period on Merseyside as the leading clubs struggled to stay in touch with the big clubs from the cotton producing towns of East Lancashire. Everton left Stanley Park and began to develop a simple enclosure on Priory Road where an entrance fee could be levied. Liverpool Ramblers also moved to new winter quarters at the cricket ground on Smithdown Road. The location contained a large flat playing pitch and a pavilion in which to change.

If Bootle were to stay in touch with their rivals an enclosed ground with good facilities was needed. The Irlam Road ground had been earmarked as a possible site for a Town Hall so a move was now inevitable. The agent of Lord Derby then offered to lease a large plot of land on Hawthorne Road. Bootle FC, along with the cricket club, slowly began to develop the allotment to suit their requirements. The council approved a new sports pavilion and put forward plans for bowling greens and tennis courts.

The Bootle fixture list for the forthcoming season was short as the club secretary had found it difficult to arrange matches with popular clubs from East Lancashire. Rivals Everton were also experiencing the same difficulties but, rather strangely, the two clubs began the season with no pre-arranged fixture. Once again the main source of local interest would be focused on the Liverpool Cup.

The draw for the Lancashire Cup presented Bootle with an away tie against Darwen. The home side, having two games to play, felt confident enough to divide their squad of players into two teams. One side travelled over to play a club game at Accrington while the remainder of the players stayed at home to face Bootle at Barley Bank. Darwen, not taking the challenge seriously, beat Bootle 14-0.

It was mid October when next Bootle assembled a decent side which was to face the reserve eleven of Aston Villa at Marsh Lane. The visitors took an early lead, which they held until the dying minutes. The Aston Villa players then disputed a late equalizer from Eyton-Jones. As the argument raged a violent rainstorm broke and sent the players running for cover leaving the game undecided.

On the 3rd of November the club played its first game on the Hawthorne Road ground. Southport was the visitors and goals from Myatt and Eyton-Jones gave Bootle a 2-1 victory. The home side later entertained their guests at the convenient placed Hawthorne Hotel.

Bootle now played two successive games in defence of the Liverpool Cup. The first game, a 2-1 win over St Mary's (Kirkdale), was played on Stanley Park. Bootle next played a home game against St Benedict's. The highlight of the tie, won 4-1 by Bootle, was the excellent display given by visiting goalkeeper, Jollife.

The New Year programme began with a visit from an exiled eleven playing under the name of "London Scottish". The large crowd, who framed the playing pitch, cheered as Wilson gave the home side a first minute lead. Back came the Scots to take a 2-1 but a late strike from Wilson earned the home side a 2-2 draw. On New Years day Bootle had a 3-1 home win over a Dumbarton X1 that was followed next day by a 4-0 defeat at the hands of Possil Park, Glasgow.

(The Dumbarton side was a detail that had been detached from the main body of the club who were playing at Blackburn on the same day. It is fair to say that, at this moment in time, the more powerful clubs from Scotland concerned themselves with money spinning visits to Lancashire and the Midlands. Here the game was more developed and larger crowds could be guaranteed.)

Three days later Bootle crossed the sea to Belfast to play local club, Cliftonville. The match was played on the Solitude Cricket ground. Heavy rain had been falling in Northern Ireland and the pitch was waterlogged. The two teams carried on regardless and very soon all the players were covered from head to foot in mud. The large crowd present, around five hundred in number, viewed the game with a good natured impartiality.

The home Captain, Davison, frequently ordered his forwards together with a firm a set of commands. Bootle, on the other hand, had the best of the game but failed to brake down the stubborn Irish defence. The game ended 0-0.

On February 23rd Queens Park Strollers paid their first visit to the new Bootle ground and gave the home side a lesson they would never forget.

The Scots lined up in a 2-2-6 formation with the forwards keeping together in pairs. The wing men kept close to each touchline and exchanged passes as they ran down the field. The two centre men were immediately supported by the swift running half backs to always give their side four men in front of the opposing goal. The Bootle backs were drawn out on the flanks which always gave the visitors an extra man in the middle. This style of play was executed with clinical efficiency by the Scots. The home fans could only look on in amazed admiration as Queens Park won the match 9-0.

Bootle now played a series of domestic fixtures. Their home ground had been slowly enclosed and the Hawthorne Hotel engaged as a temporary headquarters. However, the quest to win the Liverpool Cup now initialled a difficult away tie at Earlestown.

There was a large and hostile crowd thronging the pitch when Bootle took the field at Wargrave Road. The home side, cheered on by the vociferous crowd, inflicted a first half assault that left the visitors reeling. Goals from Dagnall (3) and Ellison gave Earlestown a 4-0 lead at the interval. Bootle, who played a little better in the second half, lost the tie 4-0. The undisguised season then drew slowly to a close with one or two minor fixtures.

Season 1884-85

During the summer Bootle signed on Job Wilding from Wrexham Olympic and the young Welshman was soon to prove a promising prospect. Building work was well in hand when 1883-FA cup winners, Blackburn Olympic, opened the new season at Hawthorne Road. The weather was fine and attendance was around eight hundred. The visitors took to the field with six of the players who had achieved the famous cup final victory over the Old Etonians.

The home side surprised their award-winning opponents by taking a first half lead thanks to a goal from Roberts. Olympic then woke up to their task and goals from Slater and Costley gave them the lead. The visitors then faded and a late goal from Hutton earned Bootle a most commendable 2-2 draw.

The Lancashire Cup draw sent Bootle to face Darwen at Barley Bank. The visitors, improving slightly on their last visit to the ground, were beaten by 7-1.

On November 1st Hawthorne Road welcomed the first visit of Everton. There was a crowd of around one thousand people lining the pitch when Bootle kicked off towards the Stanley

Road end of the field. The sides then played out a goal less first half. When the game restarted two goals from M'Gill put Everton firmly in control. With the daylight now fading into darkness, a mix up in the Everton defence led to Williams securing a goal for Bootle. Before the cheers had died down the final whistle sounded leaving Everton winners 2-1.

The annual invasion from Scotland began on New Years day with a visit from the Vale of Leven. The Dumbarton side, fatigued by the long journey, arrived late and delayed the kick off by thirty minutes. Bootle had much the better of the first half and a goal from Woodburn gave them a half time lead. The latter stages of the game, which contained a flurry of goals, were played in near darkness. Bootle is reported to have won 4-1.

Dumbarton football club was on tour in the Northwest and once again sent a representative eleven to meet Bootle at Hawthorne Road. The style of play demonstrated by the Scots, a short passing game, had yet to be seen at Bootle and was much applauded by the crowd. The opposing full backs, the Vieth brothers, caught the eye of all that witnessed the game with their collective defensive play. Nevertheless it was the home side who took the lead with a goal from Woodburn. The visitors refused to lie down and secured a 1-1 draw with a late goal from Aitken. The Scots were later entertained at the Neptune Hotel in Clayton Square, before making their way to Exchange Station where they boarded the train that would take them on the overnight journey home.

London Casuals, a top amateur side, visited Hawthorne Road during their January tour of the North The team was made up of former pupils from Westminster and Charterhouse Colleges plus one or two from Eton. The inclement weather had left the pitch resembling a quagmire so the sides agreed to restrict the play to thirty-five minutes each half.

The amateurs went off at a dash and raced into a three-goal lead before the heavy pitch began to militate against their style of play. The home side came back strongly towards the end and scored two goals. The Casuals however held out to win the game by 3-2.

Next weekend Bootle travelled to meet Southport. The visitors, after changing in the Shakespeare Hotel beat the home club 3-0. The match was played at the athletic ground which at the time stood on Sussex Road.

In February, Bootle played host to Preston North End. The Ribbleside club, undefeated all season, were now the most famous team in the kingdom and to receive a visit from them was a great honour. The Bootle executives were to be congratulated for obtaining such a fixture. There was a great interest shown by the public and the game, despite being played on a Monday afternoon, was watched by a crowd of fifteen hundred.

The visitors, fielding eight of their first team players, excited the home fans from the start with a style of play that was a joy to behold. The first goal, scored by John Goodall, was exceptional. Collecting the ball in his own half he dribbled past all the defenders and placed his shot between the Bootle uprights. The home spectators, with prolonged applause, gave the goal the recognition it deserved. Preston continued to delight the crowd and secured three more goals before Anderson scored for

Bootle, Nick Ross then added a fifth and the half time whistle sounded.

The home side, which never lost heart, began the second half with great determination but the Prestonians remained in control. Goodall scored two further goals before a late success by the home forwards made the final score. Bootle 2, Preston North End 7. The visitors later enjoyed the local hospitality at the Hawthorne Hotel before they departed for home.

The campaign to re-capture the Liverpool Cup began with a home game against Haydock St James. The Bootle side, showing one or two new faces in their line up, won the game 3-1. A round two victory over Bootle Wanderers then gave them a third round tie with Everton.

The match was played at the new home of the Everton club on Walton Breck Road. The simple enclosure, a former cricket ground, contained no facilities so the sides changed at the nearby Sandon Hotel. Everton now used the building as their club headquarters

Bootle, who won the toss, and elected to play towards the Anfield Road goal with the pronounced slope and strong breeze in their favour. The game that followed was played at a slow pace and was a rather cautious affair. Consequently no goals were scored during the allotted ninety minutes. When the referee ordered an extra half-hour of play the game burst into life. Johnstone, much to the delight of their large following, gave Bootle the lead during the first period. The goal however stung the home team into life and, with ten minutes left to play, a goal from Whittle put them level. The excitement now reached fever pitch as the three thousand spectators cheered their favourites on. With seconds remaining Parry, picking up a loose clearance, drove the ball past Harry Jackson in the Bootle goal to give Everton a 2-1 victory This was a cruel blow for a Bootle side who had acquitted themselves well throughout the game.

A strong Earlestown team awaited the visit of Bootle to their ground at Wargrave Road. Included for the first time in the Bootle line up were Vietch and Hutton two players who had been imported from Scotland. The two players made careful start as Bootle lost 3-1.

One week later the Hawthorne Road ground staged the Liverpool Cup final between Everton and Earlestown. The largest crowd yet seen on Merseyside, over five thousand people, paid for admission to the new enclosure. Earlestown, who might had been considered to be the away side, brought with them close on two thousand supporters.

Everton had the lion's share of the play but could find no way passed Champion the Earlestown goalkeeper. Midway through the second half a single goal from Simms proved to be decisive. Earlestown thus became the third team to have their name engraved on the trophy.

The return club fixture between Bootle and Everton took place at the Walton Breck Road enclosure on 7th March. A crowd of one thousand people looked on as goals from Pollock and Whittle gave Everton a 2-0 first half lead. When the team changed ends the crowd saw Bootle squander a couple of good chances before Everton increased their lead with a third goal that was scored by Richards. A late consolation goal from Woods did little to lift the Bootle spirits as they sustained their third defeat of the season at the hands of their closest rivals.

Season 1885-86

During the close season Bootle lost the services of Job Wilding when the Welshman joined Everton. The first of the pre-arranged club fixtures began with a home match with Accrington The crowd, eight hundred in all, watched Bootle surprise the visitors with a 2-1 victory.

On the 2nd of September Bootle arrived at the Sandon Hotel to prepare for the game with arch rivals Everton. The sides then made the short walk to the home enclosure and battle commenced. Job Wilding was instrumental in the build up to the first Everton goal that was scored by Gurley. The home side, watched by a crowd of one thousand, went further ahead with a goal from Farmer. The game ended in a 2-0 win for Everton.

Bootle next met a collection of ex patriot Welshmen who had established a team on Merseyside. Playing under the name of "Liverpool Cambrian" the team acquired a ground on Balmoral Road. The two clubs met here and played out a 1-1 draw.

Bootle then travelled to East Lancashire to play the second X1 of Blackburn Rovers. The match was played at the Leamington ground which, at the time, was the headquarters of the home club. The game ended in a 1-1. (Blackburn Rovers, refusing to pay a rent increase, moved to Ewood Park in 1890.)

As both clubs now had a free Saturday, Everton and Bootle agreed to participate in a hastily arranged club fixture. The game took place on the Everton ground where the rain fell in torrents as the sides took to the field. The spectators, numbering around two thousand, stood huddled together around a pitch that was totally exposed to the elements. The same applied to the people who sat on the open grandstand that had recently been added to the North side of the enclosure. Against this dismal and unsheltered backdrop, the sides kicked off.

The home side began the game kicking up the slope and took the lead with a goal from Fraser. Bootle then drew level from a corner. The kick, taken by Morris, struck Roberts on the shoulder and rebounded into the goal. A goal from Farmer then restored the Everton lead and the teams changed ends.

The rain, which continued to pour out off the sky, filled the ground with pools of water but the teams struggled on. Things looked grim for Bootle who now, along with the heavy ground, had the incline against them. With the odds stacked against them, they fought back and equalized with a goal from Roberts. The game ended in a 2-2 draw.

The month of November began with a match at the new home of the Earlestown club on the Mesnes cricket ground. The visitors, playing with ten men, produced their worst performance of the season. Looking lost in the strange environment, Bootle lost 7-4. Goal-less draws then followed at home to Davenham and away at Wrexham before a miserable month ended with a 5-2 home defeat by Darwen.

December, which was a quite month, got under way with a relaxed home and away fixture against two clubs elevens from Chester FC. The club players again divided their strength the following Saturday. One side beat Southport to advance in the Liverpool Cup while the other eleven stayed home to beat St Benedicts 5-0. The club executive, for the third week running, divided the players into two teams of equal strength. One side lost 2-1 at Davenham while, at Hawthorne Road Tranmere were beaten 3-1. The year ended with a home game against Bolton Wanderers "A".

The New Year began with a visit from the Welsh cup holders, Chirk. The game, played on a Monday, produced a disappointing attendance. Bootle won the game by 4-2.

The Liverpool Cup draw once again took Bootle to Earlestown. Their opponents, Earlestown Wanderers, were a new team who played on a narrow pitch behind a local tavern. A snow-covered pitch and a hostile crowd mattered not to the men of Bootle who scored four goals in each half to win the game 8-1.

Next day Bootle made a first ever trip to play Burnley. The visitors, arriving by train, made the short walk through the town centre and arrived at the field of combat. This turned out to be a large field known locally as Turf Moor. The area, which contained a sports pavilion, was used by the indigenous population for all their outdoor sporting and recreational events.

The match took place on the section of the moor that was directly in front of the Wellington Hotel. The playing surface, made worse by the overnight rain, was in a shocking state and the spectators were few. Bootle had several first choice players absent which affected their performance. They lost the game 3-1.

The return game between Bootle and Everton took place on the 23rd January at Hawthorne Road The visitors began the game on a pitch that was covered with soft snow and surrounded by three thousand people.

Once again the two sides proved to be well matched. The game swung from end to end until, late in the second half, Job Widing put Everton one up. Bootle then besieged the visitors' goal. The Everton defence, well marshalled by Captain George Dobson, proved defiant in the extreme. They held out until the game ended in a 1-0 win for Everton.

There was a crowd of fifteen hundred to see the return match with Earlestown at Hawthorne Road. The home side were anxious to avenge their previous heavy defeat at the hands of the visitors. This however did not prove easy. Bootle, taking an early lead found themselves level at the break. However a second half goal from Morris gave Bootle a 2-1 victory.

On February 3rd the Lancashire FA, in acknowledgement of the many fine improvements, selected the Hawthorne Road enclosure to stage the county game against Ulster. The match referee was no other than Major Marindin, the FA President. Despite the extremely cold weather a crowd of three thousand arrived to watch the play and support the appearance of home forward Eyton Jones. The visitors lost 6-0.

The home enclosure then hosted domestic fixtures with Stanley and Liverpool Ramblers before accepting a visit from the railway men of Crewe. Bootle, fielding their best crop of players, won the game 3-0.

Walton Stiles was the venue chosen to stage the Liverpool Cup semi-final between Haydock and Bootle. The vast majority of the two thousand spectators present favoured Bootle, as was evident from the cheers when the sides took the field. Bootle took an early lead when Anderson, picking up the ball in the centre, skipped through the Haydock defence to put his side one up. The same player then increased the lead before the break. Two second half goals from Morris and Gibson gave Bootle a 4-0 win. They would now face Everton in the final.

With the two leading clubs in the area participating in the final the Liverpool FA were forced to play the final on the neutral venue at Walton Stiles. The now defunct Liverpool Association had used the ground until it was taken over by Stanley FC in 1883. The present tenants enclosed the pitch with a simple fence to allow a fee to be taken at the gate. The ground, now covered with houses, once stood near to the present day Goodison Park.

Eight thousand people were reported to have paid for admission to a ground where the newspaper reporters complained about the lack of press facilities and were forced to do their work out in the open. Fortunately for all concerned, the teams kicked off in bright sunshine.

Everton began the game defending the Walton Lane end and took a first half lead with a goal from Gibson. Bootle, led by their captain Eyton Jones, attacked their opponent's goal for most of the second half but could not find a way through the solid Everton rearguard. When the final whistle was heard

Bootle had to acknowledge that they were beaten 1-0. All was not alas in vain as the proceeds of that year's competition, £130, was donated to various local charities by the committee of the Liverpool Football Association.

A chance for Bootle to quickly avenge the defeat came from a most unusual source. Liverpool Athletic Club had recently been forced to leave their home on Low Hill and relocate at Fairfield. The new stadium, which stood on Prescot Road, consisted of an almost circular running track that was a quarter of a mile in circumference. The surface was laid with cinders and the setting contained a fine gable ended grandstand. The Athletic club, in order to draw attention to this new venture, invited the local soccer clubs to take part in a tournament with a silver shield being awarded to the winners.

The contest was arranged to coincide with the Whitsun holiday and eight clubs took part. Bootle beat both St Benedicts and Oakfield Rovers to reach the final. All that now stood between them and the prize was their old rivals, Everton.

The two teams met on the evening of Whit-Monday. Mr. W H Bailey (Liverpool Ramblers) kindly accepted the invitation to officiate and by the end of the game must have surely regretted his decision. With an enthusiastic crowd of eight thousand people packing around the playing area, Bootle kicked off and immediately attacked the Everton goal with vigour. Roared on by their camp followers Bootle dominated the first moiety and led at the interval courtesy of a goal from Routledge.

Minutes into the second half a cross from Farmer was fisted out from beneath the cross bar by Galbraith in the Bootle goal. The umpire decided the ball had crossed the line and awarded a goal. The Bootle contingent, who clearly thought otherwise, appealed to Mr. Bailey to settle the matter. The official found in favour of Everton and allowed the goal to stand.

Miffed by this stroke of misfortune the avenging Bootle forwards swept up the field and besieged the opposing fortress. Routledge, following a melée in the Everton goalmouth, scored for Bootle. The umpire objected to the goal on a plea of offside and appealed to Mr. Bailey. The referee agreed with the umpire and the goal was disallowed. The Bootle players and officials strongly aired their grievances but Mr. Bailey was having none of it and waved the protests aside. The game ended 1-1 and both sides agreed to a period of extra time.

During the extension of play, Job Wilding scored the deciding goal that won the game for Everton. The Bootle executive immediately lodged a protest. They claimed that all the referees' decisions had gone in favour of their opponents and refused to concede defeat. The Athletic club responded to this resolution by with holding the prize. The matter was then placed before the Liverpool FA committee who, after much deliberation, award the shield to Everton.

Season 1886-87

During the summer months Mr. Betts, now the Bootle secretary worked tirelessly to strengthen the playing staff at the club. Job Wilding resigned from Everton along with Izatt who was formerly with Third Lanark. However, the most significant acquisition was Blackburn born John Holt who was signed from Accrington based side, Church.

The playing staff at the club was now enough to occasionally place three teams in the field. However, travelling to away matches was sometimes a problem for certain players and not always the principal contingent was available to represent the club.

During the month of August the club released an extensive programme of fixtures that had been arranged for the forthcoming season. Much to the surprise of the Bootle supporters, a game with Everton was not included.

The season got under way with a 4-1 defeat at Crewe that was followed by a 2-1 home win over Astley Bridge. The club next sent a weak side to play at Davenham while a stronger eleven remained at home and beat Manchester Wanderers.

The FA Cup draw gave Bootle a home game with Great Lever. A crowd of three thousand people watched a game that was played in a downpour. The visitors looked at home on the heavy pitch and soon raced into a 3-0 lead. The home side hit back swiftly with goals by Routledge and Woods to make the score 2-3 at the break.

When play restarted the Great Lever goal was subjected to a constant pounding. Morris twice struck the crossbar but the visitors defence held firm. John Holt was then badly hurt and had to leave the field. A late goal made the final score 4-2 in favour of Great Lever.

Providence now took a hand and Bootle received a home draw against Everton in the Liverpool Cup. The first round draw, perhaps a little premature, infected the area with its first epidemic of cup fever.

Bootle, with one week to prepare, quickly arranged a home game with Rawtenstall. The Lancashire side, visiting for a second time, beat the home side 3-1. Everton did likewise by arranging a mid-week fixture with Liverpool Police. On Saturday both sides met at Hawthorne Road.

The occasion was accompanied by sunny weather and from well before the kick-off queues of people formed up at the pay boxes. Some of he crowd, fearing the gates being locked, gained entry by scaling the hoarding and fences that surrounded the field.

The large crowd, estimated at ten thousand, presented an imposing site as they pressed hard on the ropes that surrounded the pitch. The visiting captain, Dobson, was joined in the middle by his counterpart J Rodgers. Both men protested to the referee on the ground of crowd encroachment. The Bolton official, Mr. J J Bentley noted the protest and the game began.

The cup-tie was all that the spectators could have wished for as both sides tore into their opponents. Hacking and barging was accepted from the start with no quarter being given and none asked for in return. The play, which was fast and furious, was frequently halted by the crowd who came tumbling over the ropes and onto the field of play. Bootle pressed the visitors for most of the first half but at the interval the score line was blank.

The sides, after taking refreshments on the field, restarted the game. When a long-range shot passed close to the Everton goal post the home side claimed a goal. The Bootle umpire, showing great integrity, declared the effort to have gone wide and Mr. Bentley awarded a goal kick. With twenty minutes left to play, a centre from the Everton right dropped in front the home crossbar. Harry Jackson, the home goalkeeper, unnerved by the crowd on his goal line, fumbled the ball. Before he could recover, Briscoe put Everton one up.

The Bootle captain, Eyton-Jones now rallied his troops who attacked the Everton goal but a goal line clearance from Dobson saved the day. The incident once again brought the crowd flooding onto the playing field. Once more the play was halted while the stewards and officials cleared the field and repaired the ropes. Everton, when play restarted, swept up the field and swarmed around the Bootle goal, from the fracas that followed Richards scored a second goal for Everton.

The goal knocked the heart out of Bootle as they began to play out the dying minutes of the game. With one and a half minutes still remaining, Mr. Bentley blew his whistle and awarded a throw-in. The crowd however, thinking the game was over, swarmed on to the field and chaired the Everton players towards the pavilion. The Bootle captain then appealed to Mr. Bentley to play out the full period of time but the official at once demanded that the pitch first be cleared. This was deemed to be impossible and the sides left the field.

The argument continued in the pavilion with the officials of the Liverpool FA becoming involved. Eventually the Everton team reappeared on the field. Bootle however, who were perhaps hoping for a re-match, declined to follow. The Liverpool FA allowed the score to stand and awarded the tie to Everton.

Encouraging the fans away from Anfield was proving difficult for Bootle who, on 9th October, attracted a gate of eight hundred for the visit of Accrington. On the same day over four thousand people packed into Anfield to watch the game between Everton and Bury. As games against local clubs were now becoming mundane, the committee pinned their hopes on the visit of Burslam Port Vale to produce a large crowd. Everton however captured the uncommitted local fan by offering them a chance to watch the famous Corinthians.

The prospects for the season were not helped by an early exit from the Lancashire Cup. Their opponents were Witton and the match took place at Red Lam Brow. Bootle, fearing the eligibility of certain players, placed a weak side in the field and were beaten 3-1.

A home crowd of three thousand next watched Bootle play Earlestown. The home side, after twice going behind, were level at the break thanks to goals from Anderson and Morris. A late second half goal won the game for Bootle.

Over the Christmas holiday, Bootle entertained Darwen in front of what was the largest crowd of the season. The spectators were not to be disappointed as the sides produced one of the finest football matches ever witnessed on the Hawthorne Road ground. The previous heavy defeats inflicted by the visitors were now a thing of the past and the improvement in the standard of play on Merseyside was there for all to see. The game, which continually hung in the balance, was settled by a single goal that was scored for Bootle by Izatt.

The New Year holiday proved disappointing with regards to the local response to the fixtures on offer at Hawthorne Road. The two games with Witton (Blackburn) and Stoke "A" were watched by a grand total of just three thousand people. Poor weather and local opposition through the early months of the year did little to offset the expense of travelling to both Astley Bridge and Church. Job Wilding was picked for Wales in their match with England and missed the 3-1 home victory over Blackburn Park Road.

There was a crowd of eight hundred at Hawthorne Road for the visit in February of the Druids. The home side had slightly the better of the early exchanges and led at the break with a goal from Izatt. Bootle then dominated the second half where a second goal from Izatt was followed by a brace from Morris to give them a 4-0 victory.

On March 21st a grand charity match was arranged in aid of the Bootle hospital with the opposition being provided by South

Shore, Blackpool. The elements alas were in an unfavourable mood. Despite this drawback one thousand five hundred people stood boldly out in the rain and watched the home side win 3-1.

The special Easter entertainment arranged by Mr Betts was by far the best in the area and brought large crowds flooding in to the Hawthorne Road enclosure. The Saturday visit of Glasgow Thistle (not to be confused with Partick) pulled in a crowd of three thousand who watched the home side hold the visitors to a 0-0 draw.

Easter Monday saw another bumper crowd assemble for the first ever visit to Merseyside of famous FA cup fighters, Nottingham Forest. Bootle, playing down the slope, surprised their eminent opponents by taking a first half lead with a goal from Wilding. Following the change of ends Nottingham Forest slowly took over the game and goals from Tutin and Jackson gave them a 2-1 victory.

Bootle had hoped the game with Blackburn Rovers would produce a bumper gate at Hawthorne Road but it coincided with a tempting fixture on offer at Anfield. The recent FA cup winners Aston Villa were playing a match against Everton. Blackburn Rovers, who had just relinquished the trophy, adopted a light-hearted approach to the game. Jack Hunter and Jem Ward, players with neighbours Olympic, were present in their line up while regular halfback Hugh McIntyre took over in goal.

The visitors took an early lead when the home goalkeeper misjudged a cross from the right. Minutes before the interval Morris delighted the home crowd of two thousand with an equalizing goal. From the restart Bootle took the game to their esteemed opponents and two second half goals from Job Wilding gave them a memorable 3-1 victory.

With spring now replacing winter Bootle consented to take part in a football match to celebrate the opening of a new cricket club at Garston. The home side made up of players from Stanley and Everton, played out a light hearted draw with the visitors. The Bootle season then ended with a 2-2 draw against Stanley at Walton Stiles.

Season 1887-88

Bootle pulled off the biggest coup yet seen on Merseyside by gaining the signature of the Scottish international player Andrew Watson. Moving to Merseyside after playing in the South, the Corinthian full back was invited to play for Bootle while studying for an engineering degree in Liverpool. The signing of such a quality player proved to be a most decisive factor in what was to be the most eventful season in the short history of the first Bootle Football Club.

The first game of the new season was played against neighbours Bootle Wanderers on their tight little ground at the top of Sandfield Place. The debut of Watson attracted a large crowd to a game that was played early on a warm Saturday evening. The first half was completely dominated by the visitors who, with goals from Wilding and Raid led 2-0 at the interval. Andrew Watson quickly built up an understanding with his captain Tam Veith and their collective fullback play was the most enjoyable feature of the game. The only drawback to the

Andrew Watson pictured in 1882

occasion, caused by the narrowness of the pitch, was the frequent loss of the ball into the adjoining playground of St James School. No further goals were added in the second half and Bootle won the game 2-0.

The game against Stanley was played on a warm summer's evening at Walton Stiles. Bootle took the lead with a goal from Job Wilding. Towards the end of the game the home spectators began to heckle their players and an altercation developed. The Bootle captain, fearing escalation, ended the game and led his players from the field.

The club executive now announced the signings of two new players from Scotland. The men in question, Hastings and Anderson were declared to be of "Amateur Status". This registration would make them eligible for all the major cup tournaments.

Bootle now engaged themselves in a series of money spinning mid-week games that were made possible by the long autumnal evenings. The first of these fixtures, against Halliwell of Bolton, was played in a downpour in front of a crowd of one thousand five hundred. (It must be stated that, at the time, Hawthorne Road ground offered no covered accommodation for the spectators.) The fixture provided an opportunity for both Hastings and Anderson to make their debut. Both players delighted the crowd with their skills but the only goal of the game, scored by Bootle, came from the boot of Morris.

The late August weather was anything but seasonal when Preston North End took the field at Hawthorne Road. Nevertheless a large attendance was there to welcome the professional players. Towards the end of the game the rain increased to a downpour and darkness covered the field. This did not stop the teams from providing an excellent game of football.

The visitors, in acknowledgement of the home team's vast improvement, placed their strongest eleven in the field. The Prestonians began the game playing in the direction of the Stanley Road goal. The home side, attacking strongly down the left, shocked their opponents by taking an early lead through Izatt. The goal, however, brought the visitors to life. They equalized with a goal from Ross and continued to have the better of the play. This was rewarded when the same player gave Preston the lead.

The second half opened in a torrential downpour that made the playing surface treacherous. The two sides, coping with conditions, continued to keep the crowd entertained. The visitors could not exert their authority over Bootle who twice went close to scoring. Preston, drawing on their vast experience, held firm and produced chances of their own. The final whistle left Preston 2-1 winners.

The standard of play displayed by Bootle was now worthy of the utmost of respect. This fact was displayed by the strength of the Bolton Wanderers X1 who arrived at Hawthorne Road on a bright Tuesday evening.

The visitors, watched by a healthy crowd of three thousand, went ahead with a goal from Howarth The home side then fought back with great courage and scored each side of the interval. Lewis, who gave Bootle a 2-1 victory, scored both the goals.

Injuries affected the Bootle line up when they faced Preston in the first round of the Lancashire Cup at Deepdale. The visitors, who arrived late, kicked off at 4 p.m. towards the barracks end of the ground.

Bootle again surprised the holders by taking a first minute lead courtesy of a strike from Izatt. The home crowd warmly cheered the goal. The Preston goal machine then cranked into action scoring three times before the half-time whistle. The robust play of the home side continued in the second half but Bootle met the onslaught with courage. Despite their efforts Drummond and Dewhurst scored additional goals. Bootle obtained a late goal from the boot of Hastings before the final whistle was heard. This left Preston winners 5-2.

The mid-week fixtures ended with the visit of the three time FA cup winners, Blackburn Rovers. The visitors took the lead when Watson diverted a free kick from Beresford past his own goalkeeper. More misfortune then followed when Watson was injured and had to leave the field. Blackburn, with an act of sportsmanship, allowed Anderson to replace the injured man. A goal from Lewis now put Bootle level and the sides exchanged ends.

The home side proceeded to miss a couple of good chances before misfortune struck again. The Bootle goalkeeper Allen saved a goal bound shot from Rushton. Allsop, attempting to clear, could only succeed in putting the ball through his own goal. Both sides later agreed, as darkness drew nigh, to end the game ten minutes early. This left Blackburn Rovers with a rather fortunate 2-1 victory.

The present Bootle side was, with the benefit of hindsight, the best to ever represent the club. It had now proved itself capable of holding its own with some of the best teams in the land. The club executive, by some shrewd and excellent signings, had made all this possible. Scottish born players Anderson, Hastings, Izatt and Weir had joined the club to accompany captain Tam Veith. Johnny Holt had been signed from Church. Job Wilding, along with fellow Welshmen Lewis and Morris had preformed with great distinction. All had blended in with local players such as Allsop and Jackson to give the club a sturdy and well-balanced side.

Early in October, Bootle again began their quest to recapture the Liverpool Cup. Their first opponents in the contest were from a Military background and played under the name of "The Liverpool Blues". This mysterious side, which lasted one season, lost 10-0.

The FA cup campaign got off to a controversial start with a first round game at home to Workington The local pressmen, when arriving at the pavilion, were informed of the two changes to the previously named line up of the home team as Izatt and Weir had suddenly left the club and joined rivals Everton. Morris took over from Izatt on the right wing while C Allsop took the place of Weir at the heart of the Bootle defence.

With a crowd of three thousand looking on the Cumbrians won the toss and elected to defend the pavilion goal. This decision forced the home side to face the strong sun. The visitors defended well for most of the first half but, just prior to the break, they conceded a goal that was scored by Job Wilding. The second half however, belonged entirely to the home side.

Hastings gave Bootle a second goal that was then followed by a hat trick from Lewis. A late goal from Morris completed the scoring to give Bootle a 6-0 victory.

Bootle then drew 2-2 with Witton before experiencing a rather acrimonious meeting with South Shore in the second round of the FA cup. Mr. T Duxbury, (Darwen) a prominent member of the Lancashire FA committee, took charge in the middle when the sides met at Hawthorne Road. The crowd, which took time to build up, was estimated at three thousand.

The Blackpool side showed early promise and took a first half lead with a goal from Hacking. Bootle pressed hard during the second half but the South Shore defence held firm However a late goal from Anderson brought Bootle level and the game ended 1-1.

The referee then offered the sides a period of extra time. The visitors, refusing the offer, promptly left the field. Bootle, when instructed to do so by the referee, kicked the ball between the undefended goalposts and claimed the tie. The matter was then placed before the FA committee who took the side of South Shore and ordered a re-play to take place at Blackpool.

The South Shore club played their home matches at Cow Gap Lane (today known as Waterloo Road) in the open countryside on the outskirts of the resort. The setting contained a wooden grandstand that was designed in the fashion of the day and the playing pitch was level. The dressing rooms were located above an ancient inn that was adjacent to the ground.

The FA committee, perhaps sensing the discontentment between the clubs, detailed the venerable Mr J Lewis of Blackburn to take charge in the middle. A report of the game appeared in the local newspaper. ...

"The Bootle representatives seemed in the best possible condition, and when they stepped on the field they looked fit to stand any exertion and hard work Their appearance alone was sufficient to make them favourites, and only a very few expected South Shore to win: the problem being how on earth South Shore had been able to make a draw with such an able combination at their first meeting ".

"Almost immediately after the ball was set in motion the home team burst away and a shot from Hacking went just outside the uprights. Following this, the Bootle players swarmed around the South Shore goal and in ten minutes a faint cheer announced the fact that Lewis had drawn first blood for the visitors. Try as they could the home team could not get a goal, but ten minutes after the first success of the Bootleites, a clever bit of play from Anderson, Wilding and Lewis enabled the first named to their second goal. And now the whistle sounded for half time ".

"After a very slight interval play was restarted, and the home team having the benefit of playing down their favourite end. The forwards played far better than they had previously done, and the Bootleites had a very lively quarter of an hour, but the goal was kept in tact. At the other end, Lewis was put on as third goal An appeal was made against the score, but without success "
"So strongly did the South Shore umpire appeal against the decision that the referee retired from the field, awarding the game to Bootle. This however, would have been a very ignominious ending to the match, and after some delay, the demand of the referee that the South Shore umpire should be

replaced was acceded to. Although South Shore pressed very hard they were unable to score, and by 3 goals to 0 Bootle pass into the third round of the competition" (Blackpool and Fleetwood Gazette.18-11-1887).

The draw for the third round sent Bootle to the small Lancashire village of Higher Walton. The local side, which processed an excellent playing pitch, began the game against a stiff breeze before a meagre attendance of spectators. The visitors proved to have the measure of the home side from the start. Four goals from Hastings were complemented by one each from Anderson and Morris to give Bootle a 6-0 victory.

The second round of the Liverpool Cup gave Bootle an away draw with deadly rivals, Everton The bright sunshine, which lent a hand to the occasion, brought a crowd of over twelve thousand to the Anfield enclosure. The Everton president, Mr. John Holding, obviously enjoying the occasion, entered the enclosure accompanied by a large party of local dignities. These included the Mayor of Bootle. When the party had crossed the pitch and taken their place on the open grandstand the two teams then entered the area.

The game was physical from the start with the dual between home forward George Farmer and Johnny Holt keeping the crowd entertained. Weir of Everton was the first man to take a knock that reduced him to hobbling on the wing for the rest of the game. The rampaging Bootle forward Hastings frequently threatened the Everton defence but goalkeeper Joliffe was always equal to the occasion. When half-time was called neither side had scored.

With the slope and steady breeze now in their favour, the visitors made a confident start to the second half and Joliffe was twice forced to defend his charge. Bootle continued to have the better of the play but, against the run of play, it was the home side who took the lead. Farmer scored the goal. Bootle now attacked with great purpose and Joliffe was again called upon the save from both Wilding and Hastings. The latter named Bootle player was then forced to leave the field following a clash with Weir.

Everton now finished the game strongly and added to their score with a headed goal from Gibson. Moments later the final whistle gave them a 2-0. The defeat was a big disappointment for Bootle who had once again been eliminated from the contest by their main rivals. Fate however now took a hand.

The Football Association, investigating a complaint from Bolton Wanderers, found Everton guilty of "persuading players to join them by financial inducement". They ordered the Anfield ground to be closed for one month and declared several of the Everton players to be of professional status. The Liverpool and District FA also passed judgement and forbade the Anfield club from taking any further part in the Liverpool Cup. They declared the defeat of Bootle to be invalid and reinstated them in the contest.

With their main rivals temporarily out of action, Bootle had the field very much to themselves. The weather however for the visit of Burnley was abominable The crowd, around three thousand in number, braved the elements and watched the sides fight out a 1-1 draw. The Welsh cup holders Chirk next appeared at Hawthorne Road on Christmas Eve. The game was watched by a crowd of fewer than three thousand and ended in a 1-1 draw.

The fourth round of the FA Cup took Bootle to unfamiliar territory and created a most mysterious set of circumstances. Their opponents, who hailed from Smethwick, had entered the contest for the first time. They had a ground at Wednesbury Road and played under the title of Great Bridge Unity.

In the days leading up to the game the Midland club received a telegraph from somebody who was claiming to be acting in their interest. The sender, in cloak and dagger fashion, informed the Smethwick club that certain Bootle players were ineligible for the forthcoming FA cup-tie. The two players, Anderson and Watson, who claimed to be amateurs, were in fact being paid for their services and should not be included in the line up. The informant signed himself "Smith of Oakfield".

The match was played on a sloping pitch and was watched by one thousand spectators. A local newspaper sent along a reporter who described the events in the style of the day ...

Bootle had never previously been seen in this district so it was not safe to prophesy as to the result. They travelled from Liverpool district the same morning, and are certainly a fine set of men, well built, and dressed in a costume similar to the Albion.

The visitors winning the toss set the Unity to play against the wind in the first half when Bootle certainly made good use of their first opportunity, for going quickly down the field, Fenn sent in a long shot which the Unity custodian failed to reach and it dropped just under the bar. How this came to be missed I am at a loss to understand unless he was hampered by the backs that stood in front of him. The Unity seldom became dangerous in the first half, for whenever the forwards got away they were invariably stopped by Watson, the international back, and by the aid of the wind the Unity were on the defensive the greater part of the time.

No further scoring took place in the first half, and I was quite prepared to see the Unity win at a canter now that the elements were in their favour. At first they pressed severely, but the visitors, who frequently broke away, got past the backs and registered a second goal. The Unity soon after secured a corner, and although no score resulted directly from it, it was popped through out of a scrimmage directly afterwards. There was still plenty of time for the Unity to win, but I was a little disappointed at their exhibition, and the visitors had their fair share of play in the last half, the score standing Bootle 2, and Unity 1 when the final whistle sounded.

The defence of the visitors was simply grand, and the back play of Watson was perfect. Their forwards were quick and made long shots for goal. The Unity were not as good as I expected. After the match Unity lodged a protest against Watson and some others on the ground of professionalism and until the result is known they are not out of the English competition. (The Smethwick Weekly News 24-12-1887)

The FA acknowledged the protest and promised to look into the matter. The result however would not be known until early in January on a date set down for the fifth round tie. Bootle in the meantime would have to wait.

Mr. Betts sat patiently in the pavilion beside the club telegraph and awaited news of the fifth round draw. Suddenly, at around two o'clock, the machine clicked into action and began to punch the tape. Mr. Betts deciphered the message and informed the assembly that Bootle or Great Bridge Unity had been drawn away against the Old Carthusians The news of the draw must have been disheartening for the club executive who would have hoped for money spinning home draw with Aston Villa or Preston North End.

The New Year holiday programme was to prove most lucrative for the club as large crowds flocked to Hawthorne Road. New Years Eve saw the visit of a powerful Bolton Wanderers side that attracted a crowd of six thousand. They beat the home side 2-1. Next day the annual invasion from Scotland got under way with the first time visit of The Third Lanarkshire Rifle Volunteers. The Glasgow side delighted the home crowd of four thousand people with a high standard of football before leaving with a 3-2 victory. Next day yet another four thousand people lined the ropes to welcome the arrival of Thornliebank from Glasgow. The visitors were reported to be "Manifestly out of condition owing to a ten-hour railway journey and a liberal supply of Morning dew". Thornliebank, obviously not at their best, lost 6-0.

With the overcome of the inquiry still hanging over them, the Bootle troops mobilized and set off on their long journey to London. They arrived in the capital to discover that the national committee of the FA had chosen to disregard the allegations and allow the club to proceed in the tournament. There would be ,however, a local FA committee meeting to look into the running of the club.

The Bootle side arrived at the Oval and changed in the pavilion. The sight of Andrew Watson descending the steps was warmly cheered by the home spectators in deference to his many fine games when playing for the Corinthians. There was a fashionable crowd of around three thousand on the ground as the teams lined up. Mr. J Henderson (Morpeth Harriers) and R Hetherington (Casuals) acted as umpires with the FA President, Major Marindin (Royal Engineers) taking charge in the middle.

The home side players were much taller than the visitors and their ranks bristled with both Corinthian and international players. Amongst them were AM Walters, Wreford-Brown and Neville Cobbold who were three of the most famous players of the day. Facing the bright sunshine, Bootle kicked off towards the Vauxhall end of the classical enclosure.

With three minutes played, the home side went in front. The Bootle defence failed to clear a cross from the right and Neville Cobbold drove the ball between the posts. Bootle attacked for most of the first half but still trailed at the break.

When ends were changed the visitors again pressed forward and Wreford-Brown was kept busy in the home goal. The Carthusians however looked dangerous on the break. The highlight of the game was the dual between Neville Cobbold and Johnny Holt and the crowd frequently jeered the Bootle man. Nicknaming him "Bluebottle" in allusion to his blue serge trousers, they chided him for his rough treatment of their favourite. As Bootle pushed forward, Cobbold had the last say. Picking up a long clearance, he sprinted down the field and put the home side 2-0 up. Bootle continued to fight and two excellent saves were required from Wreford-Brown before the final whistle sounded leaving them beaten 2-0.

Back on Merseyside the Bootle reserve side faced Southport High Park in the third round of the Liverpool Cup. A considerable crowd, all anxious for news from the Oval, flocked to Hawthorne Road. Their attention however was kept focussed on the field where the two sides fought out an exciting 4-4 draw. The local folk then gathered outside the pavilion. Minutes later the sad news arrived by telegraph from the Oval and the disappointed crowd dispersed.

Bootle football club now faced a local FA committee on charge of paying a certain number of their players. Dr Morley of Blackburn, President of the northern branch, chaired the meeting that took place at the Crompton Hotel in Liverpool. Also present was Morton P Betts from the London executive and all the prominent members of the Liverpool and District FA committee. Former Bootle players Izatt and Weir were called to give evidence before the committee adjourned and referred the matter to London. Two weeks later Bootle escaped with a caution.

The first team now took charge of the Liverpool Cup re-play. The game with High Park was played on their ground at Devonshire Road. A full strength Bootle proved too strong for the Southport side who were beaten 9-0. The victory left the way open for a semi-final clash with neighbours, Bootle Wanderers.

Two thousand people gathered for the game that took place on the Stanley FC ground at Walton Stiles. Bootle started like a whirlwind and first half goals from Anderson (2) Wilding and Hastings gave them a 4-0 lead. The second half was played at a much slower pace and a late consolation goal from Hooper made the final score, 4-1 in favour of Bootle.

Stanley now faced Tranmere for the right to meet Bootle in the final. The venue, which proved unpopular with the fans, was the new cricket ground at Garston. A sparse crowd of spectators watched the sides play out a 1-1 draw. The re-play, which took place in a snowstorm, was played on the Liverpool Police ground at Fairfield. The event was watched by a few hundred people and ended in a 9-1 runaway victory for Stanley

Northwich Victoria provided the opposition for the annual charity match in aid of the Bootle borough hospital. The mayor, Alderman Webster, was present in the special enclosure along with many other local dignitaries. The double admission fee, which proved unpopular, affected the gate. The game was watched by a crowd of two thousand and Bootle won, 9-0.

The popular Easter fixtures began on Good Friday with a visit of Dumbarton Athletic. There were five thousand people present when teams lined upon a pitch that was made heavy by the overnight rain. The two sides, despite the wretched conditions, strove hard to entertain. With the score standing at 2-2, a late goal from Hastings won the game for Bootle. (Playing for Dumbarton Athletic was Alex Latta, a player who later signed for Everton).

The Bootle executive arranged two matches for Easter Monday. The first game was played between the veteran players of the home club and those of their neighbours, Everton. The match, which was played in a most convivial spirit, ended in a 1-0 win for the visitors. When the players left the field many old hatchets were left buried on the pitch. The proceeds of the game were later handed to the treasurers of the local hospitals.

The Easter fixtures then ended with an afternoon visit from Nottingham Forest who had strengthened their side with guest players. The home team where quickly on the attack and took the lead with a goal from Hastings. Bootle kept up the pressure and two goals from local youth Jamison, made the score 3-0 at half time. Job Wilding added to the total before a late consolation goal made the final score 4-1 in favour of Bootle.

The club matches concluded with the first visit to Hawthorne Road of Mitchell's St George from Birmingham. The visitors, nick named "the Dragons" took the lead with a goal from Vaughan. The home side soon recovered and two goals from Woods put them ahead at the interval. A brace of goals from Devey put the Midland side ahead but Bootle fought back to force a 3-3 draw.

The season ended on a bitterly cold day with the Liverpool Cup final against Stanley. The game took place at the Liverpool athletic grounds at Fairfield and was attended by a crowd of five hundred people. Watson and Lewis were absent from the Bootle team as they kicked off against the slope.

Bootle made an amazing start. Anderson and Fenn, passing the ball between them, raced up the field and Anderson scored without a Stanley player touching the ball. This was the only goal of the half and the teams changed direction.

Early in the second half Bootle increased their lead with a hotly disputed goal from Morris The same player then scored his second and his side's third. The game then became rough and Stanley was reduced to ten men by an injury to Wright. The number was soon down to nine when W Brown was ordered from the field by the referee Mr. J J Bentley of Bolton. The game then ended in a 3-0 win for Bootle. Mr. A E Holt, the President of the Liverpool FA, was on hand to present the trophy to the Bootle captain, Tam Veith. The eventful season then ended in cheers.

Season 1888-89
The Combination

Rivals Everton had now been accepted as one of the founder members of Football League while the Bootle application had sadly been rejected. Also left out were Nottingham Forest and Sheffield Wednesday. Bootle, along with other prominent clubs, formed a combination to help secure their survival. The fixtures were not obligatory so the results could not be tabulated.

During the summer months Andrew Watson had left Bootle and returned to Glasgow. His loss was much lamented by the home fans for he was, without doubt, the finest player ever to wear the blue and white striped jersey. The man signed to replace him was McFarland from Airdrieonians. Bootle then lost the services of Johnny Holt who crossed the borough boundary and signed for Everton.

When the cricket season was over the Hawthorne Road enclosure was once again adapted for football. The portable sections of wooden seating was moved over to the eastern side of the field and positioned around the football field. This added to the permanent covered structure that was now in position along the Bedford Road edge of the ground

The new season got under way with a friendly game against Accrington. The crowd, around four thousand in number, were kept waiting for over an hour by the late arrival of the visitors. Bootle got off to a good start with a 3-1 victory. Monday evening saw the visit of Burnley and the two thousand five hundred watched the home side win 3-0.

On Saturday Bootle then travelled to play their first match in the combination. Their destination was Nantwich Road where they enjoyed a 4-1 win over the home club, Crewe Alexandra.

Next Monday evening Hawthorne Road was packed for the visit of the ever popular, Blackburn Rovers. The famous cup fighters were in the process of rebuilding their team and several players were new to their line up. The game was closely contested with chances being missed by both sides. The large crowd went home happy when a late goal from Jameison won the game for Bootle.

There were wins in the combination over Darwen and South Shore before Derby St Luke's appeared for the first time at Hawthorne Road. The Midland side, formerly St Luke's choir, had shocked the football world in 1884 by knocking Wolverhampton Wanderers out of the FA cup. The visitors astonished the home fans by playing the game with six players in the position of full back. Bootle, despite the tight defensive formation, won the game 4-2.

A 2-1 win over Halliwell Jubilee was followed by a 1-1 draw at home to Birmingham (formerly Mitchells) St George before Bootle suffered their first combination defeat of the season. Northwich Victoria beat them 3-2 at the Drill Field.

Blackburn Olympic was the next combination team to visit Hawthorne Road. The visitors, owing to a mix up with the trains, arrived with only seven members of their team. The numbers were then made up with players from the Bootle reserve. The depleted ranks of the Olympians could do little to stem the tide of pressure against them. Two goals from Anderson and one from Jamieson gave Bootle a 3-0 lead at the interval. The lost members of the Olympic team then put in an appearance and requested that the game start afresh. This however was not possible owing to the onset of darkness. When play recommenced, a second half goal from Hastings gave Bootle a 4-0 victory.

The weeks leading up to Christmas saw Bootle twice defeat Stanley, draw away at Darwen and gained revenge over Northwich with a 3-2 win at Hawthorne Road. Christmas day saw the veterans of the home club and those of Everton play a charity match in aid of the local hospital before the First X1 faced Earlestown in the afternoon. The men from the wagon town held the home side to a 0-0 draw.

On Boxing Day, all roads led to Anfield for the much-awaited clash between Bootle and Everton. Well before the time appointed for the kick off a large crowd filled the enclosure that was now well adapted to the needs of the spectator. The directors and their guests sat on open seating while the club members sat under a covered facility that had been erected along Kemlyn Road section of the ground. Behind each goal stood an open terrace that gave all customers a good view of the playing field. The setting also contained a stilted and covered press box that was positioned in the south-west corner.

With a crowd, estimated at sixteen thousand, filling the ground the teams kicked off on a pitch that had been left treacherous by the recent heavy rain. The game that followed was something of a farce as the players struggled to keep upright in the mud. The Bootle fans jeered Johnny Holt who was facing his old club for the first time. Both sides failed to overcome the ludicrous conditions and the game ended in a 0-0 draw.

Kilmarnock opened the now traditional Hogmanay holiday fixtures with visitors from Scotland. Bootle chose the game to give a debut to their recent signing, Ferguson. The new player settled in quickly and gave the home side a first half lead. The visitors came back strongly in the second half with centre forward "Bomber" Campbell proving a handful. The home side however, weathered the storm and increased their lead with a second goal from Jamieson. The game then ended in a 2-0 win for Bootle.

A cold wind was blowing when the next Scottish team arrived on New Years day. A moderate crowd assembled to meet the team representing the community of Moffat. The visitors, from a small Scottish border town, proved no match for Bootle who beat them 7-1.

The next day, a crowd of fifteen hundred welcomed the visit of Glasgow Northern who proved to be a more formidable side. When play began the two sides had opportunities to score but missed their chances. It was Bootle who eventually broke the deadlock by scoring on the hour. The Glasgow side however, still looked dangerous and forced the pace right to the end. They scored two late goals in as many minutes to steal a 2-1 victory.

Later in the month Newcastle West End put in their first appearance in the district. The visitors were the leading club on Tyneside. They had secured the services of M'Coll, Hannah and Kelso, which were three of the most promising young players in Scotland. The large crowd that gathered was stunned by the outcome of the game as Bootle demolished their opponents by a staggering score of 12 goals to 1.

The members of the local constabulary provided the opposition for the Liverpool Cup semi final. Playing under the name "Liverpool Police Athletic" the visitors drew a large crowd to Hawthorne Road that included many of their off duty officers. The boys in blue, all amateurs, found it difficult to arrest the moves of their professional opponents and conceded six goals. PC Rawsthorne, with a shot in the dying minutes. then struck the Bootle crossbar before the ball rebounded back in to play. The same player, with the next attack, drove a shot passed Jackson in the Bootle goal. In the dying moments the flying bobbie then ran through the Bootle defence and added his second before Bootle reached the final with a 6-2 victory. (Police constable Rawsthorne later joined the staff at Bootle.)

February found Bootle in the midlands for a return fixture with Birmingham St George. The game was played on an enclosure behind Mitchell's brewery in the Cape Hill district of the town. The visitors made a lively start and built up a 2-goal lead that was applauded by the home crowd. However, late goals from Davies and Marshall earned the Birmingham side a 2-2 draw.

The much-awaited return match with Everton took place on 9th March at Hawthorne Road. A previous fall of snow had been removed and the pitch coated with sawdust. One hour before the kick off people began to pour through the gates and quickly filled up the best viewing points. The spectators, when the sides took the field, numbered around seven thousand.

The opening exchanges were of a rough nature and several times did the referee have to intervene. Bootle, who took the play to the visitors, was rewarded with an early goal from Morris. The home side kept up the attack and Everton were frequently indebted to defender Nick Ross. Bootle went two up when, following a foul in the goalmouth, their forwards forced the ball home. Everton then got back in the game with a goal from Chadwick and the teams changed ends.

The match recommenced with a period of rough play. Bootle at last settled down and, amid deafening cheers, a goal from Jamieson put them 3-1 up. Everton then began to rally and a goal from Davies reduced the deficit. The visitors were now having all the game but the Bootle defence did their best to hold out. In the last minute disaster struck. Millward ran the ball through the middle and picked out Brown. The Everton man kept his composure and beat the despairing defenders to equalize. The game ended in a 3-3 draw.

A series of local club fixtures brought Bootle to the Liverpool Cup final where their opponents would be Earlestown. A crowd of five thousand, many of who had journeyed from the Wagon town, packed the chosen venue at Walton Stiles. Against a strong wind, Jamieson kicked off for Bootle.

Earlestown mounted the early pressure but it was Bootle who went ahead with a goal from Jamieson. The strong wind however was a decisive factor and it forced Bootle on to the defensive. Earlestown, with goals from Shaw and Sidderley, had a 2-1 lead at the interval. The play then changed direction.

The unfortunate Earlestown defenders had the added task of facing the torrents of rain that had started to fall. The wagon makers, showing great determination, increased their lead with a goal from Shaw. The rest of the game then belonged to Bootle. With a string of goals, four in all, they lifted the trophy with a 5-3 victory.

The Easter fixtures began on Good Friday with the visit of the football league side, Stoke. The home side began playing with the strong wind and gained a first half lead with a goal from Hastings. Second half goals from Jones and Campbell then gave Bootle a 3-0 victory.

Bootle Football Club 1889

Next day the Hawthorne Road fans welcomed the arrival of a team from Glasgow who played under the name of "Battlefield." The torpid defence of the visitors, possibly fatigued from the long rail journey, conceded a first minute goal that was scored by Jamieson. Second half goals from Hastings and Galbriath were added to the home side's total to give them a 3-0 victory.

The holiday programme was concluded with a visit from the Mariners of Grimsby. The men from the Fens made a lively start and went ahead with a goal from Riddick. Bootle nevertheless drew level with a goal from Campbell. The Lincolnshire men, after a prolonged and creditable struggle, were beaten by a late deciding goal that was scored by Hugh Galbraith.

Preston North End was both league champions and FA cup holders when they returned to Hawthorne Road on 15th April. A large crowd assembled for the opportunity of seeing the best team in the land. Unbeaten in the league the visitors had recently beaten Wolverhampton Wanderers in the cup final at the Kennington Oval.

Bootle, having kicked off, quickly conceded a goal from the boot of Jack Ross. The home side then took the game to their opponents and goals from Galbraith and Hastings gave them a half time lead. When the second half began the visitors were soon level thanks to a goal from Holmes. John Goodall then helped himself to two quick goals to give Preston a 4-2 lead. The hopes of the home fans were lifted by a late strike by Alfred Allsop but the invincibles held out to win 4-3.

Bootle and Everton met for a fourth time in a specially arranged holiday fixture that took place on Whit Monday. Of the Scottish players amongst the Bootle ranks, all but Davie Jardine had returned home for the summer and took no part in the game. The Everton team was at full strength with John Angus, a recent signing from Sunderland Albion making his debut in goal. The attendance, despite the price increase, numbered around ten thousand.

When play commenced the local players struggled to contain the Everton professionals. Jardine, who produced several good saves, was eventually beaten by a long shot from Geary. The home side continued to dominate and Chadwick scored a second goal minutes before the break. When play recommenced Geary immediately added a third. All play was now confined to the Bootle half of the field and time and time again Jardine was forced to save. Brady then beat the gallant keeper before Geary completed his hat trick to make the final score Everton 5, Bootle 0.

Season 1889-90

During the summer months a vast improvement had been made to the football section of the Hawthorne Road ground. A length of permanent terracing, capable of supporting three thousand people, had been constructed behind the goal nearest to the pavilion On the Bedford Road side eight hundred seats had been placed under the covering and more terracing added. The cricket committee had conceded an extra seven yards to allow the pitch to be increased to the width (ninety yards) now required for entrance to the FA Cup. No further development was allowed on this side of the ground.

The board of the football league had now taken charge of the combination and renamed in the Football Alliance. The new league would be run on the system already in place. It contained twelve clubs from the north and the midlands who all had aspirations of playing in the first division.

The early autumnal evenings allowed Bootle to engage the leading clubs of Lancashire in a friendly fixture. The season opened with a visit of all conquering Preston North End who were held to a draw. The club then enjoyed wins over Bolton Wanderers, Blackburn Rovers and Haliwell.

Bootle began their programme of Alliance fixtures with their first visit to Yorkshire to play Sheffield Wednesday. The visitors arrived late in the Steel town owing to a one-hour delay to their train at Godley Junction. The match was played at the home of the Wednesday club at the Olive Grove. (Sheffield Wednesday moved to Hillsborough in 1899.) The home club, after playing at several locations, settled on this ground in 1887. Metal railings surrounded the pitch and an open stand stood along the railway line that ran down one side of the enclosure. Cinders covered the flat standing area and the players changed in a marquee behind the goal.

The skies were becoming overcast when the sides kicked off at 4pm. The home side, which attacked strongly from the start, were thwarted by some excellent goal keeping by Jardine The heavens then opened and sent the crowd, two thousand in number, running from the sidelines to seek what shelter they could find. The home side looked more at home on the swamp like surface and two goals from Ingram gave them a half time lead. In the second half Bootle hit back with a goal from Morris but the home side held out for a 2-1 victory.

The next Bootle trip was to Birmingham for an Alliance match with Small Heath. The game was played on the home enclosure at Muntz Street and it ended in a 2-2 draw.

Dull weather prevailed when Newton Heath arrived at Hawthorne Road to play their first Alliance game against Bootle. The home side gave a debut to Kilner a recent new signing from Haydock. The game produced a moderate attendance who watched Bootle overwhelm the Manchester club 4-1.

Next week Bootle made their first visit to the town of Nottingham, and took on Nottingham Forest at the Gregory ground. The home side started in bright fashion and led 2-0 at the break. Bootle, who then displayed their fighting qualities, hit back hard. Goals from Galbriath and F Wood earned them a 2-2 draw.

The Cape Hill ground was the next destination where Bootle lined up to face Birmingham St George. When the sides left the pavilion the enclosure was filled with five thousand people. Struggling from the start, the visitors tried hard to contain the lively runs from the home forwards. This they failed to do and returned home beaten 5-1.

A 5-0 home win over Stanley was followed by the first ever visit of Sunderland Albion The Wearsiders, feeling the effects of their long journey, were soon trailing to a headed goal from Jamieson. This was quickly followed by a second goal from Morris. A goal by Kinaird reduced the arrears and the teams changed ends. The crowd, which had been slow to build up, had by now reached four thousand. Encouraged by their vocal support the home side settled the game with a third goal that was scored by Galbraith.

The Chuckery was the next port of call where Bootle lined up to face Walsall Town Swifts. The ground, which was a large open playing field, catered for all the sporting activities in the Walsall area. The match drew a crowd of fifteen hundred the vast majority of whom left for home disappointed when a single strike from Woods won the game for Bootle.

The visit of Alliance league leaders, Sheffield Wednesday brought a crowd of three thousand through the gates at Hawthorne Road. The home side, taking advantage of the strong wind, subjected the Yorkshire men to a first half bombardment. An early goal from Woods was followed by a brace from Jamieson. An additional goal from Morris gave Bootle a 4-0 lead at the interval. Sheffield Wednesday now had the elements in their favour and they tried to save the game. The Bootle rearguard however, did what was required of them. They restricted the visitors to a single goal as Bootle went on to win 4-1 and go top of the league.

There was around three thousand present at Hawthorne Road when Long Eaton Rangers made their one and only visit in November. The performance of the Nottinghamshire side, rooted at the bottom of the table, did little to elevate their problems. They conceded three first half goals, a hat trick from Kilner, and two from Jones in the second, to lose 5-0. Two weeks later Bootle played the return game was at Long Eaton. The match, which took place on the recreation ground, was won by Bootle.

Bootle consolidated their league position with a 7-1 win over Darwen before facing a return match with Newton Heath in Manchester. The visitors arrived at the headquarters of the home club which was in the Shears hotel. Here they changed before making their way to the field of battle. The home team played their matches at North road in the Monsall district of the town. The club had its origins in the large railway works that stood near the ground and dominated the landscape. Urged on by a crowd of four and a half thousand the home side quickly took the lead with a goal from Farman. Further goals from Doughty and Stewart saw Newton Heath to a comfortable victory 3-0.

The friendly match with Everton was played on Boxing Day. The number of people wishing to see the game proved to be greater than the enclosure could accommodate and many were refused entry. The gates at the Anfield Road end collapsed under the strain and many people viewed the match for nothing. The pitch was thick with mud as Geary kicked off down the slope for Everton. The home side enjoyed most of the early pressure which was checked by Jardine in the Bootle goal. Eventually, after thirty minutes, Alex Latta gave Everton the lead. The home side then increased their lead with a goal from Chadwick before the half time whistle was heard. Bootle now had the slope in their favour but failed to take advantage. The home side weathered the initial flurry of second half pressure and then hit back with a third goal from Latta. Everton went on to win 3-0.

The reserve elevens of both Everton and Bootle had safely seen their respective clubs through to the final of the Liverpool Cup and the first elevens now took the wheel. It was Monday evening when the two sides met for a third time at Hawthorne Road. With a crowd of ten thousand packing the ground the sides kicked off.

Everton made a confident start and several times during the first half Bootle were thankful for the dexterity of Davie Jardine. He made a series of excellent saves before Parry put Everton in front just before the break. The second half was just two minutes old went Latta doubled the Everton advantage. Edgar Chadwick then completed a hat trick to give Everton a 5-0 victory. The defeat would have been much heavier had it not been for Jardine who, on leaving the field, was cheered by both sets of supporters.

The Anfield ground shortly before the departure of Everton

Two Scottish teams made a New Year visit to Hawthorne Road the first of which was Cambuslang. The Lanarkshire side, making their first visit, were beaten 5-1. Next day Kilmarnock was beaten 5-2.

Bootle began their New Year fixtures with a game against Darwen at Barley Bank. Despite taking an early lead through Jamieson, Bootle retuned home beaten 3-1.

A long overnight rail journey was now required in order to meet Sunderland Albion. The game was played at Commercial Road in front of six thousand people. The home club was now under the patronage of the influential Lambton family and one of the sons, the honourable Fredrick Lambton, kicked off to begin the game. The home side dominated the first moiety and led 2-0 at the interval. Bootle, despite their long journey, finished the stronger of the two clubs and two second half goals from Jamieson earned them a 2-2 draw. The result was encouraging for Bootle who next week were to meet the same side in the first round of the FA cup.

There was a large crowd at Hawthorne Road when the Wearsiders put in an appearance one week later and stunned the home side with the transformation of their play. Beginning the game in style they took an early lead through Hannah. Minutes later Weir, with a hotly disputed goal, increased the visitors lead. A goal from Jamieson gave Bootle hope before a third goal from Sawers gave Sunderland Albion a 3-1 victory.

Alas for the visitors, all was not in order and keen eyes spotted an infringement. The Albion player White, was in fact M'Kechnie a recent sighing from Renton. The player was declared ineligible and Sunderland Albion was disqualified from the tournament. Bootle thus proceeded to the next round and received a home tie with Derby Midland.

The Midland team were appearing in the contest for the first time. The club had been formed to represent the large Midland Railway Company who had their headquarters in the town. The game, the only one in the area, produced a disappointing crowd of two thousand. The home side began by defending the pavilion end and took a three lead through Galbriath. The railwaymen, working up a good head of steam quickly equalized courtesy of Garden. Bootle were then reduced to ten men but a late goal from Harry Woods put them safely in to round three. The draw gave Bootle a home game with Blackburn Rovers.

Everton had been beaten at Stoke in round two so it was left to Bootle to carry the banner for Merseyside. However, a game with the cup favourites was not going to be easy. The weather was dull and drizzly as the teams lined up before an attendance of six thousand people.

The power of Blackburn Rovers was evident from the start as Jack Southworth gave them a first minute lead. Bootle, who was never in the hunt, then conceded goal after goal. Many of the home fans left early unable to watch such a one-sided contest. The standard of play demonstrated by the visitors left the home executive in no doubt as to what was required to reach the top level. Blackburn Rovers, all most without effort, won the tie 7-0.

Bootle now returned to Alliance duty and friendly matches. A 5-1 win over Birmingham St George was followed by a 3-1

Bootle v Preston North End 1891.

triumph at Haliwell before the club received a second visit from Preston North End. With no other match taking place on Merseyside the Hawthorne Road ground was packed when the sides took to the field. One or two players were absent due to other commitments the most notable being Trainor. He was playing for Wales against Scotland at Paisley. His place in the Preston goal was taken by a Spanish player named Rodriguez who was associated with St John's College, Preston.

The visitors, always welcome at Bootle, had the better of the first half and took the lead by the means of Hendrey. Bootle, who contested the game well, went further behind with a headed goal from Thompson. A late strike from Jones reduced the deficiencies before a last minute goal from Nick Ross made the game safe for Preston.

The Following Saturday, 29th March, Hawthorne Road quickly filled up for the return match with Everton. The home club presented a new player to the crowd in the form of E Howell a Welsh international from Built. Bootle were fortunate with the toss and Everton began against a strong wind and bright sunshine. Bootle put the elements to good use and led 2-0 at the interval with goals from Campbell and Howell. The crowd, which had been building up constantly, now numbered around twelve thousand. The Everton forwards, cheered on by their numerous supporters, now began to make their presence felt. With twenty minutes played, Chadwick reduced the arrears. The Bootle defence were now starting to tire as they fought against the strong wind. They conceded a late goal from Hammond to make the final score, 2-2.

Bootle attack the Stanley Road goal

Bootle then completed their Alliance fixtures with a 3-2 defeat at Grimsby Town before friendly games with Bolton Wanderers and Notts County brought the season to an end. The team had acquitted itsself well by reaching the last eight in the FA cup and finishing second in the league. The home gates for the Alliance games had proved disappointing and away trips to Grimsby and Sunderland had turned out expensive. Still there was much to be optimistic about as the cricket section took over the enclosure for the summer.

Football Alliance.

Sheffield Wednesday	22	15	2	5	70	39	32
Bootle	22	13	2	7	66	39	28
Sunderland Albion	21	12	2	7	64	39	28
Grimsby Town	22	12	2	8	58	47	26
Crewe Alexandra	22	11	2	9	68	59	24
Darwen	22	10	2	10	70	75	22
Birmingham St George	21	9	3	9	62	49	21
Newton Heath	22	9	2	11	40	44	20
Walsall Town Swifts	22	9	3	11	44	59	19
Small Heath	22	6	5	11	44	67	17
Nottingham Forest	22	6	5	11	31	62	17
Long Eaton Rangers	22	4	2	16	35	73	10

Season 1890-91

There was much turmoil experienced during the close season with players moving to and moving back from different clubs. A reshuffle amongst the committee members left Messrs Heard, Morton and Prescott effectively at the helm. Their first decision was to appoint Frank Woods as team captain and bring in Murray from Scotland. Also added to the squad was the Lancashire stalwart, Bethal Robinson who was signed from Darwen. The club however was running at a loss and for a while things looked desperate.

The season opened in the best possible manner with a visit from the biggest box office draw in the land, Preston North End. The league champions, who put out their strongest side, pulled in a crowd of over seven thousand. (Other than games with Everton, this was the largest crowd ever to watch Bootle.) With the evening sun setting over the Mersey, Dewhurst kicked off for Preston. The home side refused to be overawed by the visitors and throughout the first half they matched their every move. Both sides showed excellent form but when half time arrived neither of them had scored. The second half got off to a deafening start when a shot from Morris put Bootle ahead. The North Enders now sprang into life and a goal from Nick Ross soon brought them level. The visitors kept up the pressure and went in front with five minutes to go. Bootle made one last strenuous effort and, with seconds remaining, equalized through Thomas Wood. The final whistle was barely audible amongst the noise as the game ended 2-2.

The Alliance games began with a visit to Hawthorne Road from Nottingham Forest. The visitors, much stronger than last season, easily overcame their hosts. The home side's defensive problems were highlighted as they went down 5-1.

The club meanwhile had received a surprise offer of help from, of all clubs, Everton. The old rivalry was forgotten as their neighbours offered to promote a game to help raise some extra revenue for their cash strapped neighbours. The Hawthorne Road club gladly accepted the invitation and on Monday September 9th the two sides met at Anfield. The game was well patronised by the public and, despite an extra charge, six thousand people paid for admission. Everton lost the toss and took up position in front of the Anfield road goal and play commenced.

Everton had the best of the early exchanges and took the lead after fifteen minutes through Geary. The home side continued to dominate but were thwarted by some excellent goalkeeping from Jardine. No more goals were scored and the teams changed ends. Bootle, now with the slope against them, equalized with a goal courtesy of Murray. The Everton response was swift and a brace of goals from Chadwick put them firmly in control. The play then continued around the goal of Jardine who was frequently called on to save. Night then began to fall and, somewhere in the darkness, the visitors scored a second goal to make the final score 3-2 in favour of Everton. A sum of £135 was taken at the gate.

The problems continued with an alarming 8-3 defeat at Crewe. This resulted in many changes for the next home game against Darwen but the team, despite a vast improvement, lost 1-0.

Bootle was firmly rooted to the bottom of the league as Newton Heath arrived at Hawthorne Road. Frank Woods missed the game through injury leaving the young forward Jamieson to act as his deputy.

With a small crowd watching, the visitors kicked off. Bootle at last put a little urgency into their play and soon commanded the game. A goal from Murray and an own goal from Slater gave them a 2-0 lead at half time. The home forwards continued the bombardment and goals from Murray and Grierson added to the score. A period of rough play then ensued before Roger Doughtey was ordered off the field. The Bootle captain then pleaded for the referee to be lenient and the Newton Heath man was allowed back into the game. A late goal from Jamieson then gave Bootle a 5-0 victory.

The win briefly took Bootle off the bottom of the league before the club travelled to Nottingham. The match was played on the Town ground which was now the new home of the Nottingham Forest club. The day went badly for Bootle who lost the game 7-1. (The Nottingham club were later deducted two points for fielding an ineligible player.) Home draws with Sunderland Albion (3-3) Small Heath (1-1) was then followed by a 1-0 away defeat at Stoke.

As several of their best players were ineligible, the FA requested that the club enter their cup contest via the qualifying rounds. The first match sent Bootle to the northern border town to meet a Cumberland league side with the name of Carlisle Red Rose.

The match, which was played at Boundary Street, was won 6-1 by Bootle

The second round draw gave Bootle a home tie with Newton Heath. The Manchester club sent a weak side but it did include their regular full back pair of Powell and Mitchell The home club, despite fielding their reserve side, included several well experienced players. The day was wet and the spectators were few. The home side had the best of the play but the class of Powell and Mitchell was there for all to see. Their resistance was at last broken by McAuley whose single goal gave Bootle a victory. The Alliance team meanwhile, were away at Grimsby. The game was played on a heavy pitch and was watched by five hundred people. The home side won the game with a single goal that was scored by Walker.

With the first team on their way to Stoke the second eleven made their way to Bolton to negotiate a third round tie with Haliwell. The game was to be a most bizarre affair. The visitors took to the field on time to be faced by only five of Haliwell players. With less than twenty people watching, the tie began. Goals from Joynson and Daighton put Bootle ahead as three more players arrived. The home side then slowly built up their full complement of players and went on the win the game 4-3. The first eleven fared no better losing 1-0 at home to Stoke.

A 5-2 defeat at Darwen was closely followed by a pre-arranged mid-week game with the touring side of Cambridge University. The students, once a power in the land, were no match for the professional players of Bootle and lost 8-0.

With the festive season now upon them, Bootle languished at the bottom of the league. Wins over Derby Midland and Belfast

Distillery created little interest as did the New Year visits of Partick Thistle and Rotherham.

The Alliance games recommenced with a 4-4 draw at home to Birmingham St George and a 6-1 success over Walsall Town Swifts. A friendly game with West Bromwich Albion was well received by the fans. The midland club, sending a strong team, drew a crowd of over five thousand people. The game ended in a 0-0 draw.

On February 7th Bootle made their annual visit to Anfield to take on neighbours Everton. The game generated a wealth of local interest and thirteen thousand people packed the ground. The home side were having their best season to date and were soon expected to take the league title from Preston. Everton fielded their best possible side with only Hannah and Parry being absent from the full line up. Included in the team were former Bootle players, Campbell and Jardine. Everton took the field first followed by Bootle who received a great reception. Given little chance in hearts of fair minded people, Bootle won the toss and Geary set the game in motion

The first half was a rather tame affair in which both sides failed to score. The teams then crossed over and battle recommenced. Bootle attacked the Everton goal and a firm shot by Kilner was beaten back by Jardine. Before the keeper could recover, Murray was on hand to drive the ball past his former team mate. The goal was greeted by bouts of prolonged cheering but Everton weren't beaten yet. Chadwick was now switched inside to accompany Geary who was having a quiet game. The manoeuvre proved an instant success as the former Blackburn man put Everton level. The home side now subjected their opponents to a fuselage of heavy pressure which they gallantly resisted. Bootle goalkeeper Dunning, a recent signing from Glasgow Rangers, endeared himself to the crowd with a series of excellent saves. In the last minute the old hoodoo struck. A fierce shot from Latta found its way through the Bootle defenders and into the corner of the net to give Everton a 2-1 victory. The goal broke the hearts of the Bootle faithful who had watched the team acquit themselves with honour.

The two sides were now drawn together in the Lancashire cup. The tie, which was played two weeks later, took place at Hawthorne Road. Once again the ground was packed and the gate money swelled the Bootle coffers. Smart Arridge was back in the Bootle side while only Geary was absent for Everton. At 4 pm, the hostilities commenced

The first half proved unkind for the home side as they soon trailed to a goal from Hammond. Further misfortune then followed when a seemingly harmless shot from Chadwick deceived Dunning and rolled into the net. No further goals were added before the teams changed ends. When the second half commenced the play began to get rough and several fouls were committed. The referee, Mr Roberts, then called the two sides around him and admonished them for their behaviour before ordering Kilner off the field. John Holt quickly intervened on behalf of the Bootle man and, following an apology, Mr Roberts invited Kilner to rejoin the game. Play then resumed in an orderly manner. Everton held their lead and a late goal from Wylie made the final score 3-0 in their favour.

Wins over Stanley and Earlestown then put Bootle into the final of the Liverpool Cup which guaranteed them another money spinning game with Everton. The game was played at Hawthorne Road in the presence of 8,000 spectators. The visitors, facing a strong sun, kicked off towards the pavilion end of the ground. The visitors had the best of the first half and led 2-0 at the break. Bootle, more convincing in the second half, tried hard to save the game. A late goal from Hastings reduced the arrears but Everton lifted the trophy with a 2-1 victory.

However, things in the Alliance were not looking too good. Bootle with several difficult games to play, were next to bottom of the league. The long overnight trip to Sunderland proved to be fruitless as they returned beaten 4-1. Bootle fared no better at Small Heath where they were beaten 7-1. The season ended with a defeat at Sheffield Wednesday to leave Bootle one place off the bottom.

Stoke	22	13	7	2	57	39	33
Sunderland Albion	22	12	6	4	69	28	30
Grimsby Town	22	11	5	6	43	27	27
Birmingham St George	22	12	2	8	64	62	26
Nottingham Forest	22	9	7	6	66	39	25
Darwen	22	10	3	9	64	59	23
Walsall Town Swifts	22	9	3	10	34	61	21
Crewe Alexandra	22	8	4	10	59	67	20
Newton Heath	22	7	3	12	37	55	17
Small Heath	22	7	2	13	58	66	16
Bootle	22	3	7	12	40	61	13
Sheffield Wednesday	22	4	2	13	39	66	13

Season 1891-92

In a concerted effort to improve the line up, the Bootle committee had worked tirelessly during the close season. Throwing out their net, they drew in nine new signings. Moonie Dickson and Mullock were found in Dundee along with Graham and Lamont from Dumbarton. G W Davies (Oswestry) and J W Davies (Newton) were brought from Wales along with a man from Bangor who had the eponymous sounding name of Smart Arridge.

Bootle began the season with a match against Everton who were the new champions of the league. The match was played on an excellent Anfield playing surface in front of a crowd of seven thousand spectators. Heavy rain beat down as Moonie kicked off for Bootle and another season was underway.

Everton were the first to show and took the lead after five minutes through Latta. Bootle had a few attempts to score before play began to settle in their half of the field. Goals from Chadwick and Thompson added to the Everton tally before the whistle sounded for half time. The second half belonged entirely to Everton who, with goals from Chadwick (2) Thompson and Latta ran out winners, 7-0.

Sunderland Albion had resigned from the Alliance while Stoke and Darwen had been accepted into the top flight. The three teams who replaced them were Ardwick Lincoln City and Burton Swifts. Bootle began their programme of Alliance matches with a visit from the popular Nottingham Forest. The midland club, favourites to win the title, took the field in warm sunshine before a crowd of four thousand. The Hawthorne Road playing surface was in excellent condition which suited the style of play of the visitors. Overpowering the home side, Forest won the game 4-1.

Next Saturday Bootle travelled to Manchester for their first meeting with league newcomers, Ardwick. The club, formerly St Marks, had joined up with two teams from the Gorton area and taken over a ground on Hyde Road. Bootle changed at the Hyde Road Hotel before making their way to the ground at the top of Bennett Street. The enclosure, which stood on railway property, was packed by a crowd of six thousand people. The two teams then played out an exciting game that ended 3-3. Bootle then had a 4-3 home win over Crewe before losing 4-1 at Grimsby

On Ocotber19th Hawthorne Road received a visit from Royal Arsenal. The London side, who had recently turned professional, were importing players with the hope of becoming the first Southern team to acquire football league status. The visitors, as yet unknown on Merseyside, attracted only a small crowd. The two teams played out an entertaining match that ended 2-2. Bootle continued their Alliance fixtures with a 3-1 defeat away at newcomers, Lincoln City. A 1-0 home win over Small Heath was followed by 4-3 defeat at Crewe. The club next travelled to face league leaders Nottingham Forest at their new home at the Gregory ground. The home club had moved to the new location, situated in the Lenton area of the town, when

Top left, the Hawthorne Road ground. Top right, The Walton Stiles ground, Middle right, Site of the future Goodison Park

the site of their previous Town Ground had been taken over by the local council to build a new tram shed. The home side proved too strong for Bootle who lost 5-1. A disappointing defeat away at Walsall was followed by a home win over Burton Swifts on Christmas Day. Glasgow Northern provided the opposition on New Years Day where a one thousand crowd watched a 2-2 draw.

Heavy snow had fallen during the night before Bootle was due to face Newton Heath on January 9th. The home committee quickly engaged a large force of workmen to clear the playing area. Their efforts proved successful and, amid the high banks of snow, the game went ahead. The conditions however reduced the attendance to fifteen hundred.

The ground remained soft under foot helping the sides to produce an admirable game of football The home side pressed from the start but the sturdy defence of the "Heathens" held them at bay. At length a shot from Clarkin was beaten out by Slater in the Newton Heath goal. Before the defenders could react, the same player put Bootle one up. The goal stirred the visitors into life and, as half time approached, Donaldson headed them level. The Manchester side had slightly the better of the second half as both sides tried hard to settle the issue. The game however ended in a 1-1 draw.

The FA Cup draw gave Bootle a home game with football league side, Darwen. A fall of snow, followed by a severe frost, had left the ground in an extremely bad condition. The referee, Mr Lewis (Blackburn) arrived and inspected the pitch and, after due consideration, he declared it fit to stage a cup tie.

When play began the visitors looked at home in the conditions and quickly took the lead with a goal from Alexander. The home crowd however soon began to air their displeasure at the rough style of play implemented by the Darwen side. Their displeasure further increased when a goal from Entwistle doubled the Darwen advantage. The atmosphere further intensified when, following a rough tackle, Bootle was reduced to ten men by the loss of Dickson. The game then ended in a 2-0 win for Darwen.

The home crowd then aired their grievance against the standard of refereeing implemented by Mr Lewis. The Blackburn official was pelted with snowballs and struck by members of the crowd before he reached the safety of the pavilion. The crowd then turned their attention on the Darwen full back, McAvoy. The player was surrounded and kicked before he too reached the pavilion. The hostile crowd then surrounded the building and demanded that the Bootle executive enter a protest. The police, struggling to maintain order, sent for reinforcements from Bootle Bridewell. The extra officers soon restored order and cleared away the crowd before escorting the terrified Darwen party to the nearby Victoria Hotel. Here they changed before being further escorted to Kirkdale railway station. Here they boarded a train that would take them home.

The next home game, against Ardwick, was delayed for a long time owing to the non-appearance of Mr Lewis who had been appointed to referee the game. It was later, decided, by mutual agreement, that Everton official Mr Stockton would take charge and that play would be reduced to thirty five minutes each half. With two thousand five hundred looking on, the game at last got started.

The pent-up emotions that had been caused by the delay were soon let loose by the players as the teams strived to gain an early advantage. Both sides had their chances before Montgomery headed Bootle into the lead. Clarkin then struck the Ardwick post before the former Everton player C F Parry drove the ball past Dunning to put the Manchester side level. The two sides then quickly changed ends. Parry continued to cause problems for the home defence but Dunning proved to be in fine form. There then followed a moment of history. Moonie, racing through the defence, was tripped by Ardwick goal keeper

Douglas. Mr Stockton, following an appeal, awarded Bootle their first ever penalty kick. The kick was successfully taken by Smart Arridge who gave Bootle a 2-1 victory.

A 3-2 home win over Lincoln was followed by a difficult trip to south Yorkshire to play Sheffield Wednesday. The match, which took place at the Olive Grove, saw Bootle lose 4-1. Bootle, after losing 3-0 at Burton, then suffered a disappointing double defeat at the hands of Birmingham St George.

The London club Clapton, who were touring Lancashire, made an Easter visit to Hawthorne Road. The game however failed to

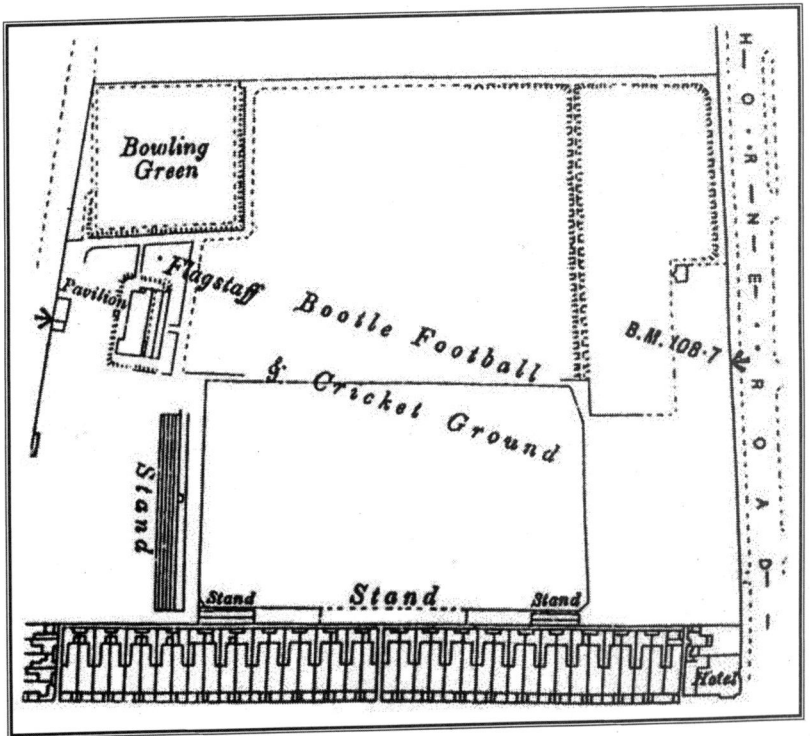

Bootle Cricket and Football Ground - 1892

The Forgotten Rivals

Hawthorne Road 1882.

create much interest and only a small number of people turned out to watch the match. The visiting goalkeeper, E H Jackson, had recently been selected to play for England in their forthcoming match against Wales. The custodian however was beaten three times in the first half. The amateur side were many times indebted to Jackson who was frequently called on to show his class. Bootle at last broke through and a further goal from Clarkin gave them a 4-0 victory

Bootle, with two home games left to play, were next to bottom of the league. Their position was considerably improved with a 6-1 win at the expense of Grimsby Town. The last game of the season, against Walsall Town Swifts, was won 3-0 to give Bootle a total of eighteen points. This put them level on points with three clubs but their goal difference was inferior to them all.

Final table.

Nottingham Forest	22	14	5	3	59	22	33
Newton Heath	22	12	7	3	69	33	31
Small Heath	22	12	5	5	53	36	29
Sheffield Wednesday	22	12	4	6	65	35	28
Burton Swifts	22	12	2	8	54	52	26
Grimsby Town	22	6	6	10	40	39	18
Crewe Alexandra	22	7	4	11	44	49	18
Ardwick	22	8	6	10	39	51	18
Bootle	22	8	2	12	42	64	18
Lincoln City	22	6	5	11	37	65	17
Walsall Town Swifts	22	6	3	13	33	59	15
Birmingham St George	22	5	3	14	34	64	13

Season 1892-93
The Final Season

The Alliance was now incorporated in to the football league and renamed Division Two. The situation now offered the clubs who would finish in the top three places, a chance to gain promotion. This could be achieved by winning a test match that would take place at the end of the season. The games would be against the clubs who were occupying the bottom three places of the first division. The four clubs at the bottom of Division two would be obliged to seek re-election.

Nottingham Forest, Newton Heath and Sheffield Wednesday had been elected to Division one while Darwen had been relegated. Birmingham St George had folded and three new teams elected to the football league. These were Burslam Port Vale, Sheffield United and Northwich Victoria.

Bootle began the campaign with a 7-0 defeat against Ardwick at Hyde Road. Next Saturday there was a four thousand crowd at Hawthorne Road to welcome the visit of Sheffield United. Bootle, with goals from Montgomery and Law, won the game 2-0.

The Lord and Lady Mayor were amongst the three thousand people who gathered the next Saturday when Burslam Port Vale arrived for a league match. The game, which was played in pleasant sunshine, was watched by a crowd of three thousand. The visitors made a lively start and took the lead with the only goal of the first half. The home side attacked for most of the second half and equalized in the last minute to gain a 1-1 draw.

Bootle then travelled to meet Burton Swifts on their ground at Peel Croft. The visitors competed well and contributed to a fine game before losing 1-0 to an own goal from Smart Arridge.

Bootle lost the next league match 1-0 against Northwich Victoria at the Drill Field before having to contemplate this year's FA cup. After being asked to take part in the qualifying rounds they received a home draw with Gorton Villa. Placing their reserve side in the field, Bootle beat the Manchester side 10-0.

Round two saw Bootle receive an away draw with Liverpool Caledonians. The home side was made up of well experienced Gaelic players who had made their home on Merseyside. The match, which was played at Woodcroft Park, Wavertree, saw Bootle exit the trophy with a 3-2 defeat.

Bootle now faced a trio of difficult league matches which began with 3-0 against Darwen at Barley Bank. Small Heath then arrived at Hawthorne Road and beat Bootle 4-1. The Potteries was the next port of call where Bootle faced Burslam Port Vale. The home side, rooted at the foot of the table, had recently moved to a new home ground at Colebridge. Bootle earned a 0-0 draw.

The next away match sent Bootle to the famous Yorkshire enclosure at Bramhall Lane to face Sheffield United. The

Cutlers proved too strong for the visitors who lost 8-3. The defeat was the heaviest of the season and it left Bootle firmly rooted at the bottom of the table.

The month of December was to prove most hectic for the club as home wins over Northwich Victoria (5-2) and Grimsby Town (3-1) made way for a New Years Eve visit from league leaders, Darwen.

Bootle in the meantime met neighbours Everton in the customary match on Boxing Day. The match, watched by a crowd of fourteen thousand, was played on the new ground of the Everton club at Goodison Park. The enclosure had been well designed with the comfort of the spectators in mind. Terraces rose up behind each goal to give the standing spectators a clear view of the field. A covered grandstand, capable of seating five thousand people, ran along one side of the pitch with two dressing rooms situated beneath. The crowd was in turn separated from the playing pitch by a strong wooden fence.

With both sides fielding their strongest team the game kicked off at the appointed time. The visitors had the better of early exchanges but failed to take advantage. Everton took a first half lead when, following good play from Hartley, Latta beat M'Loughlin in the Bootle goal. The visitors hit back in the second half and secured a well deserved equalising goal through Montgomery. The game ended in a 1-1 draw (This was the only visit to Goodison Park by Bootle football club.)

Merseyside was in the grip of winter when Darwen alighted from their train at Kirkdale station. With the memories of their previous visit fresh in their minds, the party made their way attentively along the icy pavements before arriving at the Hawthorne Road enclosure. A bleak mid-winter sight now greeted them. A mist hung over the ground and the playing surface was covered with a white blanket of hoarfrost. Nevertheless the game went a head.

A small crowd looked on as the home side overpowered their opponents from the start. A goal from Gallagher after seven minutes was followed by a first half brace from Clarkin. A second half goal from Whitehead gave brief hope to the visitors, before two goals from Grierson gave Bootle a 5-1 victory.

The cold snap showed no sigh of retreating as Bootle faced Leith Athletic the next day at Hawthorne Road. A meagre attendance looked on as both sides struggled on the icy pitch. The visitors returned to Edinburgh nursing a 2-1 defeat.

Bootle competed in just two league games during the month of January, the first of these being at Crewe. The game, which was played at Nantwich Road, saw Bootle take the lead with the only goal of the first half. The home team rallied during the second half and scored twice to achieve a 2-1 victory.

The return game with Ardwick was played the following week at Hawthorne Road before a disappointing attendance. Bootle, eager to avenge their 7-0 defeat, took an early lead courtesy of a headed goal from M'Lafferty. Further first half goals from Montgomery and Clarkin put Bootle firmly in control. The visitors, who recovered late in the game, lost 5-3.

Bootle now faced a tough task at Small Heath. The Birmingham side unbeaten at home, sat firmly on the top of the league. The game was played in front of six thousand people at Muntz Street who watched Bootle lose 6-2.

The draw for the Liverpool Cup semi-final gave Bootle a match with Liverpool and on March 11th the sides faced each other in front of five thousand people at Hawthorne Road. The visitors, members of the Lancashire League, fielded a side made up of players who had been imported from Scotland. Both sides were well received and, against the sun and wind, Grierson kicked off for Bootle. The Liverpool side, who made an uncertain start, conceded a goal in the first minute from the boot of Gallagher. The home team then increased their lead. Ross, the Liverpool goal keeper, collided with home forward Lafferty and the loose ball was hammered home by Gallagher. The Liverpool man was unable to continue and was replaced in goal by Matthew M' Queen. Shortly after the incident the game reached the half way stage and the sides changed ends. Things looked bleak for Liverpool who, with only ten men, now faced the wind and the setting sun. However they showed their fighting qualities and reduced the deficit with a goal from Harry M'Queen. Liverpool pressed on to the end but was unable to secure another goal. The game ended 2-1 in favour of Bootle.

The crowds at Hawthorne Road were now beginning to dwindle and the club had to rely on the patronage of around one thousand loyal fans. The visit of Burton Swifts produced such a number of spectators who watched the home side lift themselves off the bottom with a 3-2 win.

The number was reduced as bottom club Walsall Town Swifts arrived at Hawthorne Road the following Saturday The crowd, nine hundred in all, looked on as Bootle had their best win of the season. The midland side were outclassed from the whistle and lost 7-1. Two weeks later Bootle, without an away win all season, travelled to Walsall for the return match. The match was watched by a few hundred people who stood around the Chuckery pitch. The poor away form shown by Bootle continued as they went down 3-2.

A 2-1 home win over Crewe Alexandra improved their league position before Bootle prepared to make the long overnight journey to Lincoln. The railway company, showing much consideration, supplied a comfortable saloon carriage to enable the party to sleep during the long over night journey. The trip however proved expensive for the cash strapped club. The match, played on the John 'O Gaunt ground, saw Lincoln win 5-1.

Bootle, who were now facing re-election, had just one home game left to play. This was against the team directly above them, Lincoln City. The sides were both on seventeen points but, by a margin of ten goals, Lincoln had a far superior goal difference. The club in the meantime had to face Preston North End in the semi-final of the Lancashire Cup.

The match was played on the Liverpool ground at Anfield and it generated a gate of eight thousand that brought Bootle some much needed revenue. North End won the toss and elected to play the first half with the slope in their favour. Preston, still a force to be reckoned with, completely dominated the first period of play. When the half time whistle sounded they led 4-0. The task now proved to be beyond the Merseyside club. Despite mounting a gallant fight back they went down 6-4.
The all important return match with Lincoln City took place at

Hawthorne Road on a bright and sunny afternoon. The game however incited little interest amongst the local population and only one thousand turned up to view the proceedings. Bootle, who began the game with the sun at their backs, made a confident start. Their control of the first forty-five minutes was well expressed by two unopposed first half goals that were scored by Gallagher and Brandon. The east Midland team then made a gallant bid for safety and reduced their arrears with a goal from Moore. Nevertheless their chances of avoiding re-election were shattered by late goals from Brandon and Clarkin. The troubles of Bootle football club were eased for a while as the 4-1 victory took them to safety.

Football League Division 2.

Small Heath	22 10 1 0 57 16	7 1 3 33 19 36
Sheffield United	22 10 1 0 35 8	6 2 3 27 11 35
Darwen	22 10 0 1 45 15	4 2 5 17 21 30
Grimsby Town	22 8 1 2 25 7	7 3 0 17 34 23
Ardwick	22 6 3 2 27 14	3 0 8 18 28 21
Burton Swifts	22 7 1 3 30 18	2 1 8 17 29 20
Northwich Victoria	22 7 0 4 25 26	2 2 7 17 32 20
Bootle	22 8 1 2 35 20	0 2 9 14 43 19
Lincoln City	22 6 2 3 30 18	1 1 9 15 33 17
Crewe Alexandra	22 6 1 4 30 24	0 2 9 12 45 15
Burslam Port Vale	22 4 1 6 16 23	2 2 7 14 34 15
Walsall Town Swifts	22 4 2 5 25 24	1 1 9 12 51 13

The last appearance of the principle Bootle eleven was April 25th and it was to contest the Liverpool Cup final with Everton. The tournament had now reduced in stature and little interest was shown by the followers of Everton FC. With the first eleven of the club playing a benefit game away at Celtic the executive sent the team of players who regularly represented the club in the Combination. The weather was favourable and fifteen hundred spectators paid to watch the match.

Former Bootle favourite, Davie Jardine, was soon in action as the home side forced the pace for most of the first half. Nevertheless it was Everton who went ahead with a goal just before the interval from Reay. Within a minute of the restart, Bootle were level when, following a goalmouth scrimmage, the ball was forced over the line. Bootle had the best of the second half and Everton were frequently indebted to Jardine who made several excellent saves. Late in the game Everton broke down the right and, against the run of play, took the lead through Hartley. Bootle battled on but after the final whistle, it was Everton who received the trophy. The blue and white stripped players then solemnly made their way towards the pavilion not knowing that this was to be their final game.

The shareholders and club committee met in the pavilion at the end of the season to appraise the currant situation. The outlook however, looked gloomy. There was a moderate attendance that included, amongst others, Mr W Ward-Platt, the club auditor. Mr Heard, in the absence of the club President, took the chair and handed the floor over to Mr R E Betts a former player and now club secretary who issued the following statement ...

The directors regretted that they had to show so unfavourable a balance sheet, the cause for which they considered was due to the fact that the number of shares taken up independently of the preference shares, had not provided sufficient help that they thought. The explanation of so small a number of shares having been applied for was to be found in the delay which took place in the formation of the company. It was felt that if shares could have been allowed at the commencement of the season there would have been a much larger share list. The club had also suffered from the close proximity of the Goodison Road site, the removal of the Everton club from Anfield having told seriously against the Bootle club.

A statement of income and expenditure was then put forward which read as follows.

Income.
Gate receipts	£ 1,365.
Season Tickets	£ 54.
Donations	£ 101.
Club Draw	£ 86.

Total	£ 1,606.

Expenditure
Player's wages and fees,	£ 1,520.
Travelling Expenses,	£ 166.
Commission & Bonuses	£ 125.
Advertising & Printing	£ 154.
Police & Gatemen	£ 87.
Subscriptions to League & Association	£ 13.
Accountants Fees	£ 10.
General Charges	£ 45.

Total	£ 2,200.

It was stated, in reply to a question from the chairman, that irrespective of the shareholders, a sum of £312 was owing to various creditors. It was also stated that a further sum of £70 was outstanding in respect of the ground rent. The chairman, who advanced £5, asked if any gentleman present would help the club by lending the company any money. This was not forthcoming and the meeting subsequently agreed to a resolution to the effect that in view of the serious financial position of the club company the directors are requested to take immediate steps for considering the ways and means of carrying the club on. A vote of thanks to the chairman then brought the proceedings to a close.

The first Bootle football club, crippled by debts and lack of prospects, now went into liquidation and in doing so they became the first team ever to resign from the football league. It had proved difficult to run a football club in the shadow of what was at the time the best supported club in England. It had been a gallant effort by the people of such a small borough to challenge the hierarchy of the football world but sadly it had all ended in failure. Their place in the league was taken by Liverpool who, backed by local businessmen, quickly developed into a force to be reckoned with. Merseyside Derby matches would now be played between Everton and Liverpool but how different it might have been had Bootle AFC found themselves a rich sponsor.